Semiology

Semiology

Pierre Guiraud

translated by George Gross

London

First published in French as La Sémiologie, in the 'Que sais-je?'
series, © Presses Universitaires de France, 1971.
First published in Great Britain in 1975
Reprinted in 1988
by Routledge & Kegan Paul Ltd
Reprinted 1992 by Routledge
11 New Fetter Lane,
London EC4P 4EE
Set in Monotype Times New Roman
and printed in Great Britain by
St Edmundsbury Press Ltd
Bury St Edmunds, Suffolk
© This translation Routledge & Kegan Paul Ltd 1975
ISBN 0-415-09070-9

Contents

Foreword

Frank Kermode

English readers have lately had to accustom themselves, in fields as diverse as literary criticism, anthropology and sociology, to an unfamiliar set of terms and concepts, more or less vaguely associated with Paris. And certainly their success is attributable to the development over recent years of those methods of description and analysis that are collectively known as Structuralism. But they originate in the linguistics developed sixty years ago by the Swiss scholar Ferdinand de Saussure, and it is a curious historical accident that one of the founders of modern English method, I. A. Richards, was aware of Saussure's contribution, looked in the direction Saussure indicated, but took another road.

Had he done otherwise we might now be familiar with a Saussurian semiology different from the one which has developed in France, and which is now, with some hesitation and modification, being imported thence into England. Semiology, as Saussure projected it, is 'a science that studies the life of signs in society'. Since language is the most powerful and elaborate system of such signs, linguistics will provide a model both for the more general science and for procedures appropriate to its other departments.

Semiology has now a strong theoretical foundation, which M. Guiraud lucidly describes; but no one, I think, is quite ready to claim that it is fully formed. In particular there is still a good deal of reasonable doubt about its use, at the present stage of its development, in the analysis of the arts, including literature. It is still conceivable that it may turn out to be one of those disciplines which are of value not because the practitioners ever reach their objective—in this case a generally applicable science of signs—but by reason of casual and accidental discoveries made along the way. This used to be said of alchemy:

> And as no chemic yet th'elixir got,
>   But glorifies his pregnant pot
>   If by the way to him befall
> Some odoriferous thing, or med'cinal . . .

so we may, in the end, be grateful to semiology for providing us with new tools, yet not wish to acquire the whole kit and all the formidable manuals of advanced philosophical instruction.

However, we shall not, without some understanding of the basic principles, be able to do even this much; and here lies the value of M. Guiraud's little book. His exposition is, I think, as simple as the case allows, and the reader may decide for himself, on the basis of knowledge acquired in the early pages, whether the tactics used to validate the semiological analysis of, say, literary texts, are sound. And he will be in a position to read with more understanding the most interesting attempts yet made—which I take to be those of M. Roland Barthes—at such analysis; and to make up his mind as to whether this is the royal road to a 'science of literature' and to sciences of many other phenomena which have hitherto had to get on without them.

Along the way he will observe some reassuring landmarks. He will observe resemblances between the new *Nouvelle*

Critique and the old New Criticism. Some of the issues here discussed—for example, the polarity of 'logical' and 'affective'—were examined by Richards fifty years ago. The literary adaptation of Jungian archetypes was elaborately accomplished by Maud Bodkin in *Archetypal Patterns in Poetry*, a famous book now forty years old; and it may be that this is the part of M. Guiraud's book which will seem to the English reader least impressive as to both novelty and probability.

Nevertheless, the situation has changed in important ways. The successes of Lévi-Strauss in anthropology and Barthes in social and literary criticism; the development of new semiologically-orientated versions of Freudianism; the proliferation of 'languages' (such as advertising) which yield exciting results to this kind of systematic analysis; and above all, the renaissance of Saussure's thought in contexts where its application had been largely ignored—all these factors work powerfully to establish semiology as much more than merely a fashionable jargon. M. Guiraud is, as I say, as simple as possible; sometimes, indeed, he is terse, and sometimes he is dogmatic. He has thus performed two valuable services: first in providing a primer, secondly in offering his reader something with which, fortified by knowledge acquired from M. Guiraud himself, he may sensibly disagree.

Introduction: semiology

Semiology is the science which studies sign systems: languages, codes, sets of signals, etc. According to this definition, language is a part of semiology. However, it is generally accepted that language has a privileged and autonomous status, and this allows semiology to be defined as the study of non-linguistic sign systems, which is the definition we shall adopt here.[1]

Semiology was conceived by F. de Saussure as the science which studies the life of signs in society. Here is the much-quoted text (*Cours de linguistique générale*, p. 33):

> Language is a system of signs that expresses ideas, and is therefore comparable to writing, to the deaf-mute alphabet, to symbolic rites, to codes of good manners, to military signals, etc. It is simply the most important of these systems. *A science that studies the life of signs in society* is therefore conceivable: it would be a part of general psychology; we shall call it semiology (from the Greek *semeion*, 'sign'). Semiology

[1] *Semiology* thus defined is not to be confused with medical *semeiology* which is a study of the symptoms and natural signs (cf. p. 22 below), whereby illnesses are manifested.

would teach us what signs are made of and what laws govern their behaviour. Since this science does not yet exist, no one can say quite what it will be like, but it has a right to exist and it has a place staked out in advance. Linguistics is only a part of the general science of semiology: the laws discovered by semiology will be applicable to linguistics, and the latter will therefore find itself linked to a well-defined area within the totality of facts in the human sciences.

At roughly the same time, the American C. S. Peirce also conceived of a general theory of signs which he called *semiotics* (from *Philosophical Writings of Peirce*, p. 98):

I hope to have shown that logic in its general acceptation is merely another word for *semiotics*, a quasi-necessary or formal doctrine of signs. In describing the doctrine as 'quasi-necessary', or formal, I have in mind the fact that we observe the nature of such signs as best we can, and, on the basis of fine observations, by a process which I do not hesitate to call Abstraction, we are led to eminently necessary judgments concerning what *must be* the nature of the signs used by the scientific intellect.

Saussure emphasizes the social function of the sign, Peirce its logical function. But the two aspects are closely correlated and today the words semiology and semiotics refer to the same discipline; Europeans using the former term, Anglo-Saxons the latter.[1] Thus, as early as the

[1] *Semiology* and *semiotics* ('the general study of signs', particularly non-linguistic ones) are not to be confused with *semantics* (the study of the meaning of linguistic signifiers). As for *semasiology* (another word which belongs to linguistic terminology) it is the study of the meaning of words as opposed to *onomasiology* or study of the names which things designated can take. Unfortunately, this terminology is far from being unanimously agreed.

beginning of this century, a general theory of signs was conceived.

From the beginning, it received most attention from logicians who referred to it as *general semantics*.

Not until very recently has Saussure's programme begun to be realized; so much so that in 1964, R. Barthes (in 'Elements of Semiology', *Communications*, no. 4) could still maintain that:

> Since semiology is still in a state of under-
> development it is easy to see that there can exist no
> manual of this method of analysis; furthermore, by
> virtue of its far-reaching character (since it is to be the
> science of all sign systems), a didactic treatment of
> semiology will be possible only when such systems
> have been empirically reconstituted.

In these circumstances, it is easy to understand how risky our present undertaking is. In fact, there is disagreement even about the scope of this science. The most cautious scholars envisage no more than a study of systems of communication which use non-linguistic signals. Some, following Saussure, extend the notion of sign and code to forms of social communication such as rites, ceremonies, polite formulae, etc. Others consider that the arts and literature are modes of communication based on the use of sign systems which are also dependent on a general theory of signs. These are the three aspects of semiology which will be taken up here.

But it is clear that one can very reasonably argue that there are many other types of communication and that they, too, are parts of a semiology (or semiotic): animal communication (zoosemiotics); machine communication (cybernetics); the communication of living cells (bionics).

The scope of the present work does not permit us to tackle all these problems. We have limited ourselves to the first three. Consequently, after a general outline of the nature, form, and function of signs, the reader will find three chapters devoted to scientific and technical signs, social signs, and aesthetic signs respectively. But such an undertaking in relation to problems about which we know so little cannot but be risky. The few ideas which are analysed here cannot claim to give full coverage of a discipline which is still as fragmentary as semiology.

To conclude these introductory remarks, let us add that there has recently been created an International Association for Semiotic Studies which publishes a journal entitled *Semiotica* and a series of books on semiology.

1

Functions and 'media'

The function of the sign is to *communicate* ideas by means of *messages*. This implies an object, a thing spoken about or *referent*, *signs* and therefore a *code*, a *means* of transmission and, obviously, an *emitter* and a *receiver*.

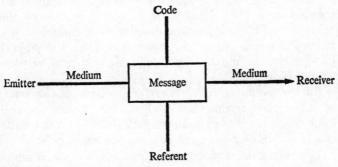

FIGURE 1

On the basis of a diagram borrowed from communication theory, R. Jakobson established his classic definition of six linguistic functions, and his analysis is still valid—*mutatis mutandis*—for all modes of communication. Furthermore, the problem of the functions of communication is linked to that of the means, the vehicle, or—to use a fashionable expression—the *medium*.

1 The functions of communication

(a) The referential function is the basis of all communication; it defines the relations between the message and the object to which it refers. The fundamental problem is to formulate true, i.e. objective, observable and verifiable, information concerning the referent.

This is the objective of logic, and of the various sciences that are codes whose essential function is to avoid any confusion between sign and thing, between message and encoded reality (see below p. 10).

(b) The emotive function defines the relations between the message and the emitter.

When we communicate—using words or any other means—we express ideas concerning the nature of the referent (this is the referential function of communication), but we can also express our attitude towards this object: good or bad, beautiful or ugly, desirable or hateful, respectable or ridiculous.

But the spontaneous expression of emotions, of character, or of social origins, etc., which are merely natural indications, is not to be confused with the use to which these can be put in order to communicate (see below p. 9).

The referential and emotive functions are the complementary yet competitive bases of communication. Hence one often refers to the 'double function of language': the one cognitive and objective, the other affective and subjective. They imply very different types of coding, the latter having its origin in stylistic variations and in connotative meanings (see below, p. 28).

The aim of a scientific code is to neutralize these variables and connotative values, while aesthetic codes bring them to life and develop them.

(c) The conative or injunctive function defines the relation between the message and the receiver, the aim of all communication being to elicit a reaction from the latter.

The injunction may be addressed either to the intelligence or to the emotional sensitivity of the receiver, and at this level one finds the same objective/subjective, cognitive/affective distinction as one does between referential and emotive functions. All sets of signals, operational programmes (work, military tactics, etc.), whose aim is to co-ordinate communal action, belong to the first category. Social and aesthetic codes whose function is to mobilize the participation of the receiver belong to the second category. The latter function has taken on immense importance because of advertising, in which the referential content of the message takes second place to the signs aimed at motivating the receiver, either by conditioning him through repetition, or by triggering off subconscious affective reactions.

(d) The poetic or aesthetic function is defined by R. Jakobson as the relation between the message and itself. This is the aesthetic function *par excellence*: in the arts, the referent is the message, which thus ceases to be the instrument of communication and becomes its object.

The arts and literature create message-objects, which as objects, and over and above the immediate signs which subtend them, are bearers of their own meaning, and belong to a specific semiology, that of stylization, hypostasis of the signifier, symbolization, etc.

(e) The phatic function affirms, maintains or halts

communication. Under this rubric R. Jakobson (*Essais de linguistique générale*, p. 217) distinguishes the signs 'the essential function of which is to establish, prolong or interrupt communication, to verify whether or not the circuit is still in operation ("Hallo, can you hear me?"), to attract the attention of the other person or to ensure that it does not vacillate ("I say, are you listening?") or in Shakespearian style: "Lend me your ears!" and at the other end of the line: "Uh-ha". The accentuation of the *contact*— the *phatic* function, as Malinowsky called it—can give rise to a profuse ritual exchange, even to whole dialogues whose sole aim is to prolong the conversation.'

The phatic function plays a very important part in all forms of communion (see below, p. 14): rites, solemn occasions, ceremonies; speeches, harangues; family conversations or amorous exchanges, in which the content of the communication is less important than the fact of being there and of affirming one's membership of the group.

The same words, the same gestures are repeated; the same stories are reiterated. This makes the communication absurd or unbearable to the outsider, but renders it euphoric for the 'participant' who 'is involved'—and unpleasant if and when he ceases to be involved.

The referent of the phatic message is the communication itself; just as the referent of the poetic message is the message itself, and that of the emotive message is the emitter.

(f) The metalinguistic function defines the meaning of any signs which might not be understood by the receiver. For example, a word is put in inverted commas or is specified: 'semeiology, in the medical sense of the term'. The metalinguistic function thus refers one back to the code from which the sign takes its meaning. It plays a considerable role in all the arts; 'writing' is a signal of the code. The word *democracy* has different meanings according to the code in

which it is used; similarly, a portrait leads to different interpretations according to its style: romantic, realist, surrealist, cubist, etc. The choice of vehicle or *medium* stems from the metalinguistic function also. The frame of a painting or the cover of a book highlights the nature of the code; the title of a work of art refers to the code adopted much more often than to the content of the message. A coal shovel outside an exhibition or museum takes on an aesthetic meaning, and here the referent of the message is the code itself.

(g) Understanding and feeling. The various functions which have just been described are concurrent; in one and the same message they can be found in varying proportions. The dominant function depends on the type of communication (see pp. 15ff, below).

The two principal modes of semiological expression are the referential (objective, cognitive) function and the emotive (subjective, expressive) function. They stand in antithetical opposition to one another to such an extent that the notion of a 'double function' of language can be extended to all modes of signification. In fact, *understanding* and *feeling*, mind and soul, constitute the two poles of our experience and correspond to modes of perception which are not only opposed but are inversely proportional, so that one could define *emotion* as an incapacity to understand: love, pain, surprise, fear, etc., inhibit the intellect, which is incapable of comprehending what is happening. The artist and the poet are unable to explain their art just as we are unable to *explain* why we are overwhelmed by the curve of a shoulder, a silly expression, or a reflection on the water.

Comprehension is exercised on an object; emotion on a subject. But above all to *com-prehend*, 'to put together', *intel-ligere*, 'to bind together', is an act of organization, an ordering of sensations perceived, whereas emotion is a disordering and an overwhelming of the senses.

Two entirely different modes of perception—and consequently of meaning—are involved. The characteristics of the logical sign and of the expressive sign can be tabulated in two columns of opposing terms as shown in Table 1 (cf. chapter 2).

TABLE 1

The logical sign	The expressive sign
conventional	natural
arbitrary	motivated
homological	analogical
objective	subjective
rational	affective
abstract	concrete
general	singular
transitive	immanent
selective	total

Of course, we are dealing with tendencies, and these properties are relative (a sign is—as we shall see—*more or less* conventional, *more or less* arbitrary). Nevertheless, they fall into two principal modes of signification which correspond to the *science/arts* polarity.

Consequently, there is mutual repulsion both between logical signs and emotion, and between expressive signs and comprehension. The semiological modes of intellectual knowledge have no bearing on affective experience, and vice versa. This is what makes the scientific study of affective phenomena so difficult and so precarious, given the impossibility of defining and structuring (i.e. of comprehending) terms such as *passion*, *desire*, or *emotion*.

Under the entry *consciousness*, Lalande's *Vocabulaire de la philosophie* has: 'Consciousness cannot be defined; we know what consciousness is but we cannot provide an unequivocal definition for others of what we ourselves are able to grasp clearly'; and further: 'We become less and less conscious as we gradually fall asleep . . . and we become more and more conscious when a noise wakes us gently.'

This definition, which Valéry must have had in mind when he wrote *La Jeune Parque*, explains the inability of logical signs to signify psychic experience. It is the basis of all the arts, which by their very nature are wedded to the iconic and analogical modes of signification. Their function is not to make us *understand* the sensations perceived by placing them in a network of objective relations, but to make us *experience* them by presenting us with an imitation of the perceived reality.

This marked polarity between objective experience and subjective experience, between intellect and affectivity, between knowledge and feeling, between the sciences and the arts, is the dominant characteristic of our 'intellectual' culture, whereas 'popular' or 'archaic' thought tends to confuse the two planes.

The ancient 'sciences', such as medicine or alchemy, are 'arts' to the extent that their content is ill-understood. Science progressively invades the domain of the arts, while the arts extend into the realm of the unconscious; astronomy pushes astrology back into the art of divination, and the arts which are ousted by science reclaim unexplored territories.

In this context of the opposition between logical and technological codes on the one hand, and modes of affective and poetic expression on the other, one may note the mixed ambiguous nature of the codes of social life in the huge domain of what is referred to today by the ambitious and still premature term: the 'human sciences'.

(h) Meaning and information. There are three types of code according to whether the signs stand in a logical

relation of exclusion, of inclusion, or of intersection. These correspond, respectively, to the diacritical (distinctive), taxonomic (classificatory), and semantic (signifying) functions (see Figure 2).

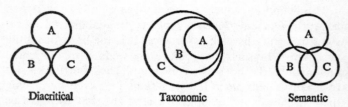

FIGURE 2

The function of a phonological system (and of most signal systems) is of a purely diacritical kind, to the extent that there is no relation between the relevant characteristics. Knowing that a phoneme is *labial* tells us nothing about the tone (*voiced* or *unvoiced*) because tone and articulation are independent; the system has maximum information, but the signs have no meaning. Meaning stems, in fact, from relation.

A taxonomic system, on the other hand, integrates the signs into a system of relations which are necessary, unidirectional and inclusive: *mammal* necessarily implies *vertebrate*. The latter adds no information to the former.

The lexical system, in which signs are in an intersecting relationship, includes both meaning and information. *Leaves* are generally *green* (which is a constitutive of their meaning), but not all leaves are green and not all green objects are leaves (which defines the information potential). Thus, a classical painter is free to depict leaves as green, yellow or purple. But other systems exist: one in which leaves would be necessarily and only green, and one in which they could be anything.

The more meaningful a code is, the more it is constrained,

structured and socialized; and vice versa. Now, the *information content* of a message and its corollary *redundancy* (or wasted information) are objective, measurable properties. The greater the redundancy, the more the communication is significant, closed, socialized and codified; the lower the redundancy, the greater the information and the more open, individualized and decodified the communication. In this perspective modern science and technology can be considered as part of increasingly codified systems and the arts as part of increasingly decodified systems.

This structuring or 'codification' of the system raises the problem of the relations of the receiver to the communication from the double standpoint of the message and of the emitter.

(i) Attention and participation. The receiver of a message must decode it, must reconstruct its meaning on the basis of signs each of which carry elements of that meaning, i.e. indications concerning the relation of each sign with the others. Thus, a jigsaw is a message whose meaning (the picture) we reconstruct by replacing the various pieces according to the clues offered by lines, colours and shapes. The greater the number and precision of such clues, the easier it is to do. That is why it is difficult to put together a jigsaw if the bits are weakly differentiated. But a difficult puzzle is more interesting to the extent that it requires greater *attention* on the part of the player (in decoding and interpreting).

For the same reason an activity which is too highly programmed—e.g. conveyor-belt work or cramming for examinations—is uninteresting. The same is true of any art in which stereotyped rhetoric makes interpretation too easy, and of any overcoded message in which redundancy causes the receiver's attention and interest to flag.

But this notion of 'interest' on the part of the receiver

must be better defined. *Attention,* as we have just defined it, is a measure of the interest which the object of the message (referent) holds for the receiver. This interest is of an intellectual kind and it stems from the pleasure obtained in reconstructing and interpreting it. The purely affective interest felt by the receiver by virtue of the mere fact of being in communication with the sender is of quite a different order: here the *intellectual element* of attention is *minimal.* Such is the nature of communication between lovers: it is wholly phatic (see above, p. 7) and its words, gestures, behaviour, have no aim other than affirming and maintaining a form of communication which gives the lovers the impression of living at the same rhythm, of 'fusing into a single being.'

This *communion* between participants takes on great importance in the collective forms of communication: religious and political ceremonies, spectacles, speeches, etc. Songs, dances or parades, are aimed at creating unity amongst the participants responding to the same pace or rhythm. Their content is secondary. The military or political harangue carries hardly any information, and doubtless should contain the least possible amount, since the object of the exercise is to rally the participants round a leader or an ideal.

Affective *communion* is comparable with practical *collaboration* which is constituted by co-ordination and synchronization of two or more persons working together. This, too, depends upon a codification and socialization of the message at the expense of its information content.

Attention (which is cognitive) should not be confused with *communion* (which is affective), or with *collaboration* (which is practical). In fact, they are inversely proportional: communion (and collaboration) demand relaxation of attention and are therefore related to antinomic coding systems.

2 The 'media'

In Anglo-Saxon semiology *medium* is used to designate the various means of communication. A *medium*, therefore, implies that the sign has a substance[1] and, furthermore, it implies that this substance itself has a support and a vehicle. And it is clear that the nature, the structure and the function of the code are closely linked to the *medium*, and this is also true of the various functions which we have just described. The present volume contains a brief inventory of the principal *media* and of their coding system. For the moment, it may be useful to discuss some of the general problems posed by the irruption of new *media* into our culture. To this end, a few words about Marshall McLuhan's ideas are in order.[2]

According to McLuhan, the *media* are extensions of our senses and our functions: the wheel an extension of the foot, writing an extension of sight, clothes an extension of the skin, electronic circuits an extension of the central nervous system, etc. They modify—and often revolutionize—our relations with our environment. Now, this relation between man and his environment (which includes other people) is inherently more important than its immediate effects or product. As a consequence, it is not difficult to understand that what is important in industrialization (by which we mean the mechanization of work) is less the product (cars, fridges, tubes of toothpaste) of the said work than the very nature of the work itself: fragmentation of the task, elimination of initiative or decision making on the part

[1] It would be more precise to say 'matter' or 'supports', because in modern linguistics, the word *substance* is used to designate the intrinsic properties of the signified or of the signifier. In this perspective, the sounds *o*, *m*, constitute the substance of the signifier *homme* [the 'h' and 'e' are silent in the French here]; and 'masculinity' is the substance of the corresponding signified.

[2] Cf. M. McLuhan, *Understanding Media*, New York, 1964.

of the worker. By the same token, the various TV programmes and their contents are of little account when
compared with the entirely new modes of knowledge implied
by the mere existence of television. What is significant is less
the actual content of the news 'bulletin' than the simple fact
that the audience—particularly children—is receptive, and
that this receptive mode quite transforms its relation to the
traditional *media*—the book, the school, the museum. The
televised message has a finality which is not so much a
function of its actual referential content as of its relation
between the sensory receiver and the referent. According to
a by now hackneyed formula of McLuhan's: 'The *medium* is
the message'.

Few will dispute McLuhan's claim that writing, then
printing, then the press and today TV have transformed our
culture. Fewer perhaps will agree with the more arguable
aspects of his brief analysis. Be that as it may, McLuhan's
account has the merit of rescuing these issues from the
hitherto exclusive clutches of philosophical and political
polemicists.

McLuhan divides the *media* into *hot* and *cool*, words
referring to what, in technical terms, is designated by the
'temperature' of the information or, photographically
speaking, the 'definition' of the image. For a given message,
the greater the number of the elements of conformation, the
denser is the informational substance and the *hotter* the
message. The inverse of this is also true. The temperature
of the message is not to be confused with its referential
content: a message is hotter or cooler as a function of the
extent to which it offers a greater or lesser number of
elements for decoding, irrespective of wealth or poverty of
the signified itself. A portrait is hot and a caricature is
'cool'. A photo and a movie film are hot while a TV shot is
cool in so far as the latter has fewer points per image. The
minuet and the waltz are hot in so far as their basic steps are

set by the code, whereas the twist is cool. The spoken word is cooler than the written word and ideographic writing is cooler than alphabetic writing.

The temperature of the message is linked to the 'participation'[1] of the receiver who has to interpret the message and, consequently, to supply certain informational elements which the message lacks. In a hot message the meaning is delivered in the message itself, whilst in a cold one it is furnished to a greater or lesser extent by the receiver who, in this way, is implicated in the communication. Thus a particularly hot assembly line schedule supplies the worker with all the information he needs for his work and by that very token denies him any choice decision or 'participation'. At the other end of the scale, you have, for example, the rules, recipes and pedagogical code of the artisan's technique. From this angle, science is hot and the arts are cool. Our western culture is hot, 'primitive' or 'under-developed' cultures are cool, urban life hot, country life cool.

Now, according to McLuhan, we are in transition from a hot to a cool culture; and the reason for this is that a mutation is taking place in the media—more specifically books are being replaced by TV and mechanization by automation, figurative by non-figurative arts, etc. The corollary of this is augmented participation by the individual and a new type of society which in certain respects is akin to the tribal life of cool cultures.

As far as the present author is concerned a *distinguo* is required with respect to the opposition which McLuhan establishes between our *hot* type of modern western culture and *cool* archaic cultures. Semiologically there are two types of experience: cognitive and affective experience. The former is in no way reducible to the latter (and vice versa); on the contrary they are inversely proportional (see above, p. 9).

---

[1] 'Participation', as McLuhan conceives of it, is related to what we referred to above as *attention*.

For us, therefore, it follows that in a given culture there is an inverse relation between knowledge and affectivity. We have, furthermore, to distinguish between the individual and the collective: that which is individual defines our differences, that which is collective defines our similarities with others. The two domains are once again inversely proportional, given that the more different we are, the less similar we are. Utilizing this dual criterion, we can divide the semiological field of our experience as shown schematically in Figure 3.

	Intellect	Affectivity	
Individual differences	–	+	Decodification Attention
Social similarities	+	–	Codification Communion Collaboration
	Sciences	Arts	

FIGURE 3

The greater the extent to which knowledge is codified and socialized, the more affective experience tends to be individualized. In the light of this framework, our culture rates as an overheated intellectual experience; individual attention is more and more restricted and creative initiative more and more impoverished. It is not that the individual is less intelligent in this culture, but that more and more of his knowledge is supplied to him by codes, sciences, programmes, etc. As a corollary to this, affective experience is more and more decodified, that is, richer, more abundant and diverse, but hence divested of meaning. Modern man's diet of knowledge is well-ordered but it is off-course where matters of desire are concerned. The semiology of our arts attests to this fact. Non-figurative (and thus designified) arts, in fact, represent a decodified and desocialized type of affective experience. These arts are characterized by realism. As for the stereotyped mass-culture versions (westerns, strip cartoons, thrillers, tin-pan alley, etc.) of 'naïve', 'archaic' or 'popular' art, they are not art-forms at all, but 'divertimenti'. They have a symbolic function the aim of which is to stage-manage certain affective situations and desires which are strictly coded, and decked out in meanings which they lack in real life.

The same applies to our games; these are mimed performances of individual or social action (see below, p. 83). These games are of two kinds: 'realistic' and 'symbolic'. To highly socialized action there correspond strictly codified games. This is a characteristic of most modern sport and is increasingly the case as far as social games like bridge and chess are concerned. As a corollary to this, the de-individualization of action and the resultant frustration are compensated for by our amusements, which re-introduce freedom and individual initiative into our lives in the guise of do-it-yourself kits for house or garden, foreign travel, dancing, etc. The verbs *to play*, on the one hand, and *to enjoy oneself* on the other, are expressions of this opposition. The two aesthetic functions correspond to the two functions of play (realistic representation and symbolic compensation), but the relation is inverted to the extent that the former signify affective experience and the latter signify rational praxis. Codified games and individualized amusements correspond to socialized, scientific, and cognitive experience. Weakly structured, representational, non-figurative arts, and aesthetic, rigorously codified entertainments correspond to individualized aesthetic and affective experience.

Clearly, these arts have quite a different meaning in the two cultures. In a highly codified art such as that of our Middle Ages, 'realism' reflects life, while the fantastic and the marvellous reflect the dream. In the decodified art of today, this is reversed: 'abstract' art reflects our real affective life, while the sentimental romance, the West End comedy, the best-seller, symbolize our desires. The same is true of social codes which, wherever they are effective, reflect a specific state of social reality with its values and its hierarchies; but where, on the other hand, they break loose from social reality they are no more than the manifestation of a will to power, a mere semblance.

The same analysis can be applied both to the codes of individual forms of social life (insignia, uniforms, protocols), and to collective codes (rites, festivals, ceremonies). Our modern society is characterized by a rigorously structured economy based on a great diversity of specialized activities; as a corollary to this we find a de-structuring of social codes. Economic and social codes stand in the same inversely proportional ratio as the logical and the affective codes. The more any practical activity is coded, the more the social framework of that same activity is decoded. Social structuring compensates for economic de-structuring; and the deficit of being produces an increase of seeming.

It is striking that functions which are but little differentiated as far as practical activity is concerned remain all the more attached to the social signs which give them their identity: uniforms make the general, the judge, the archbishop, the academician or the Burmese fakir; but for the engineer, doctor, or architect it is a different story. The doctors took off their medieval pointed hats as medicine became a highly codified and specialized science. Teachers and academics are still hesitant to cast off their regalia.

Thus, the various codes and their modes and degrees of codification are related. The structuring of knowledge leads to the structuring of games and of economic and technological codes; and to a concomitant de-structuring of arts, amusements and social codes. The ensemble is engendered by a perceptual code defined by the complementary and antithetical relation between affective and cognitive codes. The totality of these structures makes up a cultural system in which all parts are interrelated, and in which any alteration of the perceptive structure (intellect/affect)—that is to say, the mode of apperception of reality—leads to a re-structuring of the system as a whole. That is why it is inverted in 'archaic' cultures, where the relation between cognitive and affective experience is different. To the extent that the advent of new *media* modifies that relation it is easy to grant McLuhan that they constitute the key to the whole cultural system.

But these matters are still ill-understood, and the reader is entitled to question such ambitious and premature syntheses. Our aim here has been to point out the importance—indeed the primacy—of semiological phenomena by demonstrating that any culture can be defined as a system (or more precisely, a set of systems) of communication.

2

Signification: form and substance of the sign

1 Sign and signification

A sign is a stimulus—that is, a perceptible substance—the mental image of which is associated in our minds with that of another stimulus. The function of the former stimulus is to evoke the latter with a view to communication.

(1) COMMUNICATION

The foregoing definition excludes natural indications. Of course, in ordinary parlance one says that clouds are a sign of rain, smoke a sign of fire; but in such cases semiology withholds the status of sign because the cloud-laden sky has no intention of communication any more than has the wrongdoer or the hunted animal when they leave unwitting traces of their presence.

Such indications can, however, be used as signs: the clouds on television weather charts, or the description (in linguistic or other terms) of fingerprints sent out by the police. A sign is always marked by an intention of communicating something meaningful.

Nevertheless, there is a deep affinity between communication, defined in this way, and perception. Perception can rightly be thought of as a 'communication' between energy-emitting sensory reality and our sense organs acting as receivers. It is worth while giving some thought to the curious terminology which uses one and the same term (i.e. *sens*) to designate both the *meaning* (sens) of the signs (or of things) and the *senses* (sens). This is so because from the point of view of archaic etymology *sentir*, 'to direct', means 'to put into line' (and hence into communication) the perceived object and the sense organs: the *sens* (physical capacity) for an acoustic sensation is hearing, and the *sens* (that which is perceived) of hearing is an acoustic sensation.

These, however, are merely natural indications, and we shall use the word *sign* as the mark of an intention to communicate a meaning.

This intention, however, may well be unconscious, a fact which considerably extends the range of semiology. In the visible world, ancient or 'prelogical' cultures see messages from the beyond, from the gods, or from their ancestors; and much of their lore and their behaviour is founded upon the interpretation of such signs. Contemporary psychoanalysis stakes its claim in this vast domain. While it is true that medical 'semiology' is purely a study of the natural indices of pathology, psychosomatics, by contrast, sees in such symptoms reactions which are destined to communicate information, desires which the subject is not able to express any other way. Psychoanalysis—particularly Lacan's school—considers the manifestations of the unconscious as a mode of communication and a language. Parapsychology, too, postulates the notion of subliminal messages which are not conscious. These notions have been taken up by literary criticism, the study of myth, the psychosociology of behaviour, propaganda, advertising, etc., under the heading of 'depth psychology', and semiology must take this into account.

It is evident, however, that traffic signals and psychosomatics stem from profoundly different sign-systems and modes of communication. Nevertheless, in both cases we are faced with *signs* which, as is true of all signs, have two aspects: a *signifier* and a *signified*, to which we have to add a mode of signification or relation between the two.

(2) CODIFICATION

The relation between signifier and signified is always conventional; it is the result of an agreement among those who use them. This is also true in the case of motivated signs (see below) or of natural indications used as signs. The convention may be implicit or explicit, and this is one of the (flexible) boundaries which separate technical codes from poetic codes.

This analysis has been developed by linguistics but it is true, *mutatis mutandis*, for all sign-systems. But the notion of convention—particularly that of implicit convention—is relative. There are degrees of convention: it can be more or less strong, more or less unanimous, more or less constraining.

It is quasi-absolute in a highway code, in chemical or algebraic formulae, etc. It is strong in the rules of good manners, in the techniques of the theatre, in the more or less orthodox and explicit rules of rhetoric, etc. But the relation between signifier and signified may be much more intuitive, vague and subjective. Signification is more or less *codified*, and ultimately we are left with open systems which scarcely merit the designation 'code' but are merely systems of hermeneutic interpretation. Here, too, we have the frontier between *logics* and *poetics*; though it is true that certain poetic systems are, as we shall see, highly codified. What is fundamental is the notion of a *more or less* codified sign or system of signs.

Codification, in fact, is an agreement among the users of a sign: they recognize the relation between the signifier and the signified and respect it in practice. Such agreement may be more or less inclusive and more or less precise. Thus a *monosemic* sign is more precise than a *polysemic* sign (see below, p. 27). Objective *denotation* is more precise than subjective *connotation* (see below, p. 28); an *explicit* sign is more precise than an implicit one, and a *conscious* sign more precise than an unconscious one.

The greater the imprecision of the convention, the more the value of the sign varies according to the different users.

The convention, furthermore, has a statistical character: it depends on the number of individuals in a given group who recognize and accept it. The more precise and widespread the convention, the more the sign is codified.

Codification, inasmuch as its origin is implicit, is a process: usage renders the sign more precise and extends the convention. In this way the sign becomes codified. It can also become decodified.

In the course of this process it is difficult to trace the limit at which a stimulus acquires (or loses) the status of an explicit sign. This relativity of the sign is common to most of the operational concepts of semiology; depending on each particular case, signs are *more or less* motivated, and sign systems *more or less* structured, etc. (cf. below, p. 30).

(3) MOTIVATION

The sign, therefore, is based on a conventional relation (which may be a stronger or a weaker one) between the signifier and the signified. Two main types of relation can be distinguished according to whether the relation is motivated or unmotivated (the latter is also known as *arbitrary*).

Motivation is a natural relation between the signifier and the signified, a relation which is in their nature, their substance or their form; it is analogical in the first case, homological in the second (cf. below, p. 33). The terms extrinsic and intrinsic are also used sometimes.

Analogy may be *metaphorical* or *metonymic* according to whether the properties common to signifier and signified enable one to assimilate the former to the latter, or, on the other hand, whether they are linked by a bond of contiguity in space or time. Just as there are degrees of convention, so there are degrees of analogy: it may be more or less strong and more or less immediately evident. In its strongest form analogy is a *representation*: the photograph, the portrait, the dramatic performance, etc. But the iconic value of the representation is generally of a more schematic or abstract nature, as in the case of a map, a plan, or a traffic sign.

Motivation does not exclude convention: the schematized diagram of a barrier which heralds a level-crossing is, despite its iconic value, a conventional sign which the users of the code can neither alter nor replace.

It will, however, be understood that motivation frees the sign from convention, and that the extreme case of this is exemplified by purely representational signs functioning completely outside any pre-existing convention. Such is the case when new meanings are created by an open poetic system. But these new signs are rapidly codified and absorbed by the system.

The weaker the motivation, the more constraining the convention has to be; and in extreme cases it alone is able to ensure the efficacy of a sign in which there is no perceptible relation between signifier and signified. The sign is then said to be non-motivated and arbitrary.

Many terminologies—particularly those of Anglo-Saxon extraction—distinguish motivated from arbitrary signs by using the *icon* (i.e. image) for the former and *symbol* for the latter; hence mathematical *symbols* or *symbolic* logic. This convention, however, has the serious disadvantage of introducing a confusion into the usage of the word *symbol*. Traditionally, in fact, a *symbol* 'represents a thing by virtue of an analogical correspondence between them' (Lalande), and is therefore iconographic by nature. It is in this sense that we shall use the word symbol. Where its meaning is explicit, as is the case in modern science, the sign is generally arbitrary, for any analogical relation would incur the danger of altering the meaning by transferring on to the signified the properties of the signifier.

But very often the specific principle of a sign is motivated, although historical evolution tends to obliterate that motivation. And to the extent that the original motivation is no longer perceived, the sign comes to function by virtue of convention alone. This is true of most of the signs of articulated language, but also of many signs in symbolic, mantic, or protocol systems and other social codes. Like languages, therefore, such semiological systems have a double frame of reference according to whether they are considered diachronically from the point of view of their history and origin, or synchronically from the perspective of their functioning in a given culture.

(4) MONOSEMIC AND POLYSEMIC MEANING

In theory, for communication to be effective, for each signified there should be one signifier and one only, and vice versa. This is the case for scientific languages, signalling systems and logical codes in general (cf. above, p. 10).

In practice, there are numerous systems in which a signifier can refer to several signifieds, and vice versa. This is true of poetic codes in which convention is weak, iconic function highly developed, and the sign open.

As far as articulated language is concerned, polysemic meaning is the rule, and this is so because it seems that one is dealing not so much with one code as with an aggregate of superimposed and interlocking codes. Doubtless there are no polysemic codes as such, but rather systems of expression which simultaneously include several codes. Nevertheless, the resultant possibility of choice is the basis of style. To the extent that the emitter has a variety of possibilities for the formulation of his message, his choice becomes significant.

(5) DENOTATION AND CONNOTATION

The distinction between *connotation* and *denotation* is related to the above instance of choice. Denotation is constituted by the signified conceived objectively as such. Connotative meanings express subjective values attached to the sign by virtue of its form and of its function: a word in 'slang', in 'poetic' diction or in 'scientific' jargon connotes the signifier which it expresses; so does a 'hypocoristic' or 'affective' locution. A uniform denotes rank and function; it connotes the prestige and authority attached to rank and function.

Denotation and connotation constitute two fundamental yet opposed modes of signification; and, although in most messages they are found in combination, these messages can be categorized according to whether they are predominantly denotative or connotative. The sciences belong to the denotative type, and arts to the connotative.

Scientific codes, being essentially monosemic, eliminate possibilities of stylistic and connotative variation which abound in poetic codes. In a chemical or an algebraic formula stylistic variants are virtually nil or, at most, extremely limited, whereas a painter can treat a portrait in a realist, impressionist or cubist code, or any other. Here, too, the polysemia of the signs is a consequence of the variety of the codes. And this superimposition of semiological systems is a characteristic of modern western culture.

The polysemic nature of the signs is not to be confused

with that of the message. The ambiguity of the polysemic sign is in fact resolved by the content, and in a message the sign has in principle only one meaning. But it can happen that this plurality of possible meanings is implied in the message. We shall return to this fundamental problem (cf. below, p. 33).

(6) MATTER, SUBSTANCE, FORM

A sign has substance and form. Thus in the traditional meaning of these terms the substance of the traffic light 'stop' sign is an electrical optical signal, and in form it is a red disc.

However, since Hjelmslev, modern linguistics has adopted another point of view and another terminology. The red disc which defines the sign itself constitutes the *substance*; as to the *form*, it is defined as the relation of the signal to the other signals of the system—in this case the possible alternatives of green or amber. Consequently, another term has to be used to designate the optical or electrical nature of the signal; one could use the term *matter* or material substrate.

Conceived in this way, the opposition between *form* and *substance* takes on new epistemological value. In particular, it enables the distinction to be made between the substance and form of the signifier on the one hand, and on the other, the substance and form of the signified. According to this terminology the substance of the signified is defined by the underlying concept or idea; in the case of the word *cat* the abstract idea of *felinity* constitutes the substance of the signified, and its form is in the conceptual system in which it is opposed to 'kitten', 'dog' or 'man'.

So far the substantive properties of the sign have been considered. Its form, i.e. the way it takes its place in a system, remains to be studied.

2 The form of the sign

(1) THE SYSTEM

Semiologists distinguish *systematic* from *a-systematic* procedures of signification: according to the definition by E. Buyssens taken up by G. Mounin (*Systèmes non-linguistiques au XX siècle*, p. 178):

> Signalling procedures are *systematic* if their messages can be broken down into stable, constant signs: such is the case of the highway code with its discs, rectangles and triangles constituting a well-defined family of signs. But there are a-systematic procedures: an advertising poster using form and colour to publicize a brand of washing powder, or even a series of different posters used in succession for the same purpose.

While we subscribe to this definition, we should be inclined to qualify it slightly: it is, in particular, not certain that the elements of an advertising poster are as 'a-systematic' as is suggested. The study of rhetoric, for example, gives detailed analyses of the rules of a 'portrait' or a 'description', and such rules are respected in both painting and literature. The colour and style of hair, the shape and colour of the eyes, and the distance between them are surely elements of a system which has been shown to be highly structured and constraining, as in religious iconography. As for the poster, the choice of colours, size and graphics appears to obey a determinism which is much stricter than one might think at first sight. It is doubtless one of the main tasks of semiology to establish the existence of systems in apparently a-systematic modes of signification.

There are, furthermore, several types of system: 'a set of stable and constant signs' is not a linguist's definition, for in linguistics a system is an ensemble in which the signs are interdependent.

From this point of view it seems that a distinction must be made between systems with or without syntax. On a traffic sign combining a parking circle, a bar indicating prohibition and a lorry there is a mere accumulation of signs. The same is true of a hotel guide which indicates the presence of a telephone, bathroom, and breakfast service by means of a simple juxtaposition of signs without any relation between them. Our decimal system of numerals, on the other hand, does constitute a system in the linguistic sense of the term: it contains syntactical rules and the ten numerals are, moreover, interdependent. In the hotel guide the absence of the sign 'telephone' does not modify the value of the sign 'bathroom', whereas a system of numerals with a different base (5, 6, 8) would use different combinations to express the numbers signified. In a collection of shopkeepers' signs, similarly, there is no interdependence between the *cobbler's boot*, the *golden gloves* or the *basket of flowers*, whereas in heraldry there certainly are sets of elements: escutcheons, quarterings, bars; and a syntax to the extent, for example, that the divisions of a quarter (sinister or dexter, chief, centre or point) are significant.[1]

It is, furthermore, useful to distinguish two main types of syntax: temporal and spatial. In articulated language, optical signals and music, the signs stand in a temporal relation to one another; in painting, drawing and the different modes of graphic representation the relation is spatial. Many systems are mixed: dance, cinema, etc.

In this way we can distinguish *a-systematic ensembles* from *systems* with a *morphology*, that is with stable constant signs organized in categories; *a-syntaxic* from *syntaxic* ensembles, in which morphological classes take on their value by virtue of their position in the message; temporal, spatial and mixed syntaxes.

[1] *Le Blason* (Heraldry), 'Que sais-je?' series, no. 336, PUF.

(2) ARTICULATION

The problem of articulation is linked to that of structure. A message is articulated if it can be broken down into elements which are themselves significant. All semiotic entities must be significant. Thus the lorry on the traffic sign can be broken down into wheels, chassis, cabin, etc., but the presence of these elements does not modify the sign. On the other hand, the absence of a jacket or its permutation with a jersey changes the significance of the way someone is dressed.

From this point of view, language is in a special position among sign systems in that it has a *double articulation*. In fact, a message can firstly be reduced to morphemes (roots, affixes, endings) each of which corresponds to a particular signified. Next, the morphemes can be analysed into phonemes. The permutation of the phoneme corresponds to change of meaning (rang/sang; rage/sage; rot/sot, etc.); but, as can be seen from these examples, the r/s opposition has no fixed semantic correlation, whereas the opposition between *ruler*, *washer*, *hirer*, etc., on the one hand, and on the other, *ruling*, *washing*, *hiring*, etc., does correspond to the same semantic opposition: 'agent/result of action'.

The two articulations are not to be thought of in terms of syntactical levels. In fact, several levels can be distinguished in the first articulation: sentence, preposition, syntagm, word, morpheme; but each of these complex signs are simply successive combinations of the basic signs which carry the elements of meaning that are picked up at each level. At the second articulation, these semantic components are no longer present; the function of phonemes is to differentiate between and hence to distinguish the morphemes, but the phonemes themselves are not meaningful.

The double articulation is not to be confused with levels

of reading or cross-coding; if Charles Bovary's cap takes on a meaning (Bovary's clumsiness) this is the result of another (literary) code independent of the linguistic or iconographic code in which the meaning was first signified.

It is, in general, thought that the double articulation is a property found exclusively in articulated languages and that it distinguishes them from all other sign systems.[1] In fact it has been primarily the different systems of technical communication that have been studied from this point of view. But it would perhaps not be impossible to apply this notion to poetic codes as I have defined them above (cf. p. 7). The code of musical notation is doubly articulated; as is that of most dances, it seems.

(3) HOMOLOGY

Until now, we have applied the notion of articulation to signifiers. But the signifieds may also be articulated. And when both are articulated the two systems may or may not correspond.

In fact, a set of signifiers can be reduced to conceptual elements which form a system of opposed traits. Thus *horse* is opposed to *mare* by the trait *masculine/feminine*. This opposition is not, as it happens, reflected by the signifiers; but it can be in words of the type *lion/lioness*; *tiger/tigress*; *sorcerer/sorceress*, etc. In such cases, the articulation of the signifiers corresponds to that of the signified; there is an *homology* between them.

This *homology* may extend to an entire system. For example, the names of the vertical avenues and the horizontal streets of New York numbered according to their natural succession constitute a system of signification based

---

[1] G. Mounin has shown that the system of telephone numbers is doubly articulated (cf. G. Mounin, *Problèmes théoriques de la traduction*, p. 121). But such codes seem very exceptional.

on the homology between the signifying structure and the signified structure.

Homology is a *structural analogy*: the signifiers have the same relation among themselves as have the signified, whereas *analogy* (in the strict sense) is substantial. Homology does not exclude analogy, and the two can be combined. Thus the extensive system which in popular parlance assimilates the human to the animal is both homological and analogical. *Mane* and *hair*, *snout* and *nose*, *paws* and *hands* or *feet*, *claws* and *finger-nails* taken term by term are in an analogical relation, whilst the two systems are homological.

Theoretically, signifiers and signifieds may or may not be structured, giving four combinations in all. In each of these cases the signs (or parts of signs) may be arbitrary or analogically motivated. When the two ensembles are structured, the signs may be arbitrary to the extent that the two structures do not correspond. If they do correspond they are homologous. They may also be analogous. An *ad hoc* example may help: small metal or plastic clips are sometimes used at parties to help one recognize one's glass. Often they are in the form of an animal, and each guest receives one. In most cases, there is no relation either between the various insignia or between each clip and the person or glass to which it is allocated. But one could easily invent a system of signifiers divided into categories such as *mammals*, *birds*, *reptiles*, which might even be part of a wider system in which animals might be opposed to plants, etc. One could, similarly, add other characteristics such as colours. Thus classified the clips might be distributed arbitrarily; or one can imagine a classification of drinks with or without correspondence between the two systems. Thus 'men' might have an *animal*, 'women' a *plant*, 'alcoholic drinks' might be *red* or *yellow*, 'non-alcoholic drinks' *blue* or *yellow*, etc. One could, furthermore, set up an analogy by allocating *warm* colours to 'alcoholic drinks' and *cold* colours to 'non-alcoholic' ones.

Most of our sciences and much of our knowledge is based on such systems: the signifiers constitute a class of elements which are articulated, i.e. enter into certain types of relation, whereas the signifieds form a homological structure. Theoretically and etymologically (i.e. originally) the signified reality is structured, and afterwards names are allocated by constructing a system of homologous signifiers which are preferably not contaminated by analogy. In practice, one searches reality for a similarly structured system which one utilizes as a signifying system: the faculties of the soul are named after bodily functions, social organization after celestial configurations, etc. The signifying system is then a grid which one applies to the signified reality and which gives it its form.

Science proceeds in this way when it *borrows a model* from a neighbouring science. It is what is done when a text is *interpreted* by clamping a Freudian, Marxist or existentialist grid on to *Phèdre* or *Les Fleurs du Mal*. Most pre-modern knowledge is of this kind. The analysis of such 'primitive thinking' demonstrates all the pitfalls of this method, for analogy is productive only to the extent that the signifying system slices up reality according to real relations (see below, p. 59). Organizing and naming human society using the model of the stars is useful in so far as the relations between stars are precise, objective, stable and verifiable; but to do this is to risk petrifying human relations and attributing to them properties which are entirely foreign to them. And when celestial reality has itself been named on the basis of a bestiary, the three systems exchange and confuse their values. For there always follows the 'poetic' moment in which the signs are taken for the things. This recurrence of analogy has been remarkably demonstrated by Lévi-Strauss. He has shown, for example, how totemic systems are, essentially, methods of arbitrary naming and classification whose function is purely demarcational, but whose substance rubs off on to the signified by attributing to it, on the basis of analogy, properties which are not its own (cf. Lévi-Strauss, *The Savage Mind*). This is why the meaning of myths 'cannot be attributed to the isolated elements of which they are composed but to the manner in which these elements are combined'; to their form and not to their substance, Hjelmslev would say (see above, p. 29).

In a similar way, Michel Foucault contrasts pre-classical knowledge which founds meaning on the resemblance between the signifier and the signified, with modern science which signifies only the ontological relation which determines meaning (*Les Mots et les choses*, p. 44):

> The ensemble of knowledge and techniques which makes signs speak and enables us to discover their meaning, will be called hermeneutics; the ensemble of knowledge and techniques which enable us to distinguish where the signs are, to define what it is that makes them into signs and to learn the laws of their links and sequences, will be called semiology. The sixteenth century superimposed semiology and hermeneutics in the form of similitude. To seek meaning is to bring resemblances to light. To seek the law of signs is to discover things which are similar. The grammar of beings is their exegesis. And the language which they speak tells nothing more than the syntax which binds them.

This distribution between two fundamental modes of signification—analogical and homological—is the key to our scientific culture. It enables one to distinguish science from traditional knowledge, and arts from sciences.

3 Modes of communication

Let us imagine a policeman at a cross-roads: he has a uniform; he regulates the traffic; he shows me the way to the station on a map. We have three types of communication here: the uniform tells me the identity of the person; his hand movements tell me when to stop or go; the map informs me of the lie of the land. In the first instance communication concerns being, in the second action, in the third knowledge. We shall call these respectively *indication*, *injunction* and *representation*.

Now let us take up these three examples in a different situation. Our policeman puts on his uniform to go to the wedding of his cousin in Corsica; he regulates the flow of 'traffic' at the annual Police Parade; he paints a primitivist picture of a policeman helping a blind man.

The same signs have a different meaning in the two situations. In the first case the uniform is simply the index of a social function, but in the second it expresses the desire to demonstrate participation in a supposedly honourable profession and to mark the solemnity of the ceremony. In the case of the parade, similarly, it is not a question of really regulating the traffic, but of symbolically miming the supposed coherence, rigour, impassibility and necessity of his job. The picture, finally, does not merely present us with a policeman but informs us of how the artist sees and judges him, highlighting the policeman's goodness and his devotion to the community. In other words, in the three former cases what we have is an objective communication which bears only on the nature of the situation. In the three others, the emitter expresses a judgment on the situation, a judgment which he wishes to share with the receiver. To each of these six situations correspond particular modes and means of communication (see Table 2).

These terms are adopted here only for the sake of con-

TABLE 2

	Being	Acting	Knowing	
Objective logical codes	Insignia	Signals	Science	Denotation Attention
Subjective aesthetic codes	Fashions Customs Behaviour	Rites Festivals Games	Arts and literature	Connotation Participation
	Indication	Injunction	Representation	

venience and for the purposes of this exposition, and in view of the absence of an agreed terminology. Furthermore, it is clear that while some systems can be contained within this framework, the majority go beyond it and utilize mixed complex signs. Nevertheless, this schema does distinguish clearly between the two cardinal categories of signs corresponding to what linguists call 'the dual function of language': on the one hand, the signs of objectivized and rationalized intelligibility; and on the other hand, those of expressivity, subjective emotion and desire. One of the characteristics of our modern western culture is to separate these two planes of our experience; they tend to get confused, on the other hand, in archaic prelogical cultures in which the patterns of action (hunting, warfare, agriculture, etc.) are ritualized and in which arts and techniques are not demarcated from one another.

The conditions of communication pose another problem. The communication, in fact, includes a message (and its vehicle), a sender and a receiver, a referent and a code (cf. above, p. 5). The presence or absence of each of these elements determines specific types of communication.

The message and the receiver are necessarily present, but the sender may be absent, as in the case, for example, of the sender of a letter. The code is generally absent as it has been memorized by the users; one may, however, use the code in the form of a dictionary in the case of a translation, or in the case of a cryptographic message one may use a decoding grid. But the codes differ primarily in that they do or do not imply the presence of the sender and of the referent. Articulated language, gestures, bodily signals, or fashions in clothes necessitate the presence of the emitter, who is himself (or herself) the vehicle of the message. And here the fundamental constraint is the co-presence of sender and receiver. But the message may be transcribed into another vehicle: writing or gramophone recording. There is no need to emphasize the importance of this liberation from the emitter. The principal phases of this liberation are the invention of writing, that of the printing press, and today the various audio-visual techniques.

Another problem is posed by the presence or absence of the referent which may itself be the bearer of the message. Such is the case of indications such as felling marks on trees, insignia, guild signs, hallmarks and most signals. The referent may also be the emitter designating himself by means of insignia or dress. In the arts of imitation which are images of the referent, it is this image which is the bearer of the imprint and indications of signification. But the signification functions at a second level at which it is conditioned by the limits of the code of representation. Dramatic or pictorial representation of a ceremony (a consecration, a marriage, etc.) conditions the form of the ceremonial indications. In this respect, silent cinema should be compared with 'the talkies'; the former, unable to reproduce voices, transfers signification to gestures, mime and costume. Similarly, the semiology of composition is very different according to whether a picture does or does not have perspective: the centre of the picture is not in the same place, the size of the characters does not have the same significance.

In general, the poorer the mode of representation is, the greater the codification of the signs.

4 Meaning: codes and hermeneutics

Dictionaries give us two definitions of the word *meaning*: 'idea which a sign represents' and 'idea to which the object of a thought can be referred'. There is the meaning of the word *life* and the meaning of 'life' itself: i.e. what 'life' means, what does it add up to, what does it mean? In the Middle Ages there were two words, *le sens* (Latin *sensus*), i.e. immediate meaning which is apparent to the senses, and *sen* (Germ. *sinno*, 'direction') which designates the aim of the meaning, i.e. what it is getting at. Linguistic evolution has unfortunately confused the two forms, and if it has not quite conflated the two meanings, it has at least seriously obscured their limits—and by the same token it has confused the limits of the two semiologies.

At the beginning of *Madame Bovary*, Flaubert describes his hero's monstrous cap; he does so by means of words, and these words could be transcribed by an illustrator into a picture made of lines and colours. Words and picture are signs the meaning of which is this cap. But the cap in its turn has a meaning: it is the sign of Charles's clumsiness, his lack of taste, his gaucheness in his relations with his friends.

The cap is thus both the signified meaning and the signifying sign. But the meaning does not stop there: Charles's clumsiness is the sign of his relations with Emma; his relations with Emma are the sign of a certain form of marriage; which in turn is the sign of a cultural situation, etc.

The meaning is a relation, and this relation envelops each meaning in a new meaning. Thus if semiology is to be the science of signs it encompasses all knowledge and all experience, for everything is a sign: everything is signified and everything is signifier.

Our example postulates a distinction between two types of sign. The words designate the cap, the picture represents it; that is their explicit function, which they carry out (each according to a different technique) by virtue of a system of conventions which assures the readers' agreement. However, when we say that the cap is the mark of awkwardness we are dealing with a sign of quite a different kind. There is no code which necessitates that this *cap* should be the sign of 'clumsiness and bad taste', and, furthermore, agreement among readers is far from unanimous: some may even, perhaps, find it admirable and may consider Charles to be the victim of misunderstanding. It is a matter of interpretation.

In the first case, we are dealing with a *code*, that is to say, a system of explicit social conventions; in the second, a *hermeneutics*, a system of implicit, latent and purely contingent signs. It is not that the latter are neither conventionalized nor social, but they are so in a looser, more obscure and often unconscious way. Thus, the metal boot indicating a shoemaker's shop, the drawing of a boot in a catalogue, the military boot as insignia of a cavalry regiment, etc., belong to a code; on the other hand, the boot belonging to cousin Gontran who takes himself to be a gentleman farmer, the boot belonging to the concierge's son who is a member of the Hell's Angels, or the one belonging to the lady on the fifth floor who is a drawing-room equestrienne, are so many variants of a latent *hermeneutics* which, in our culture, associates boots with ideas of 'social prestige', 'command', 'virility', etc.

Thus, the message presents two levels of signification: a technical one based on one of the codes; and a poetic one engendered by the receiver using a system or systems of implicit interpretation which, by virtue of usage, are *more or less* socialized and conventionalized. And as a consensus comes to be established, little by little, as to the meaning of such signs, so it is legitimate to consider that they acquire, at the same slow pace, the status of a technical code. While it is true that the relation between the aesthetic object and its signification must be implicitly and immediately evident, nevertheless to the extent that this evidence is recognized and accepted, the sign is taken over and repeated, and its value becomes conventionalized: the *eye* is the 'mirror of the soul', the *neck* is the sign of the 'life force', etc., and the painter capitalizes on these conventions when he enlarges his model's eye or tapers out her neck. Such rhetorics, 'styles of writing', are codes; the same is true of mantic ritual in which each sign or combination of signs has an invariant conventional meaning for the initiated.

But the technical codes signify a system of real, observable objective and verifiable (or supposedly verifiable) relations, whereas aesthetic codes create imaginary representations whose value as signs stems from the extent to which they justify their claim to mirror the created world. The aesthetic message is the analogue of the surreal, of the invisible, the ineffable, or of a reality which technical signs are unable, or have so far been unable, to express: that is to say to observe, verify and allocate a conventional and unanimously accepted sign to. Logical meaning is entirely coded, locked up in and virtually contained in the code, whereas aesthetic representation is never more than partially coded and remains a relational field which is more or less open to the free interpretation of the receiver.

This degree of coding clearly varies with period, culture and genre. In the cowboy film, for example, characters, situations and behaviour are all highly conventionalized.

There are those technical codes the function of which is to signify rational experience; and there are poetic codes, the function of which is to create an imaginary universe through which an irrational experience—or in any case one which is outside the province of technical signs—is signified. And, finally, beyond the conventionalized poetic codes there is the entire domain of a hermeneutics dealing with new relations which are outside all conventions, or with unconscious conventions, or, finally, with obsolete conventions whose meanings have got lost and which therefore escape us.

In the long run, all these systems return to language, since anything that is signified, in no matter what way, can be expressed in words: one can describe a picture, a festival, a map, a chemical formula, a dream. That is why it is not surprising to find, in language, all kinds of signs and all forms of signification.

The problem—which is quite arbitrary and merely a matter of definition—is to decide what are the limits of the competence of a semiology. For some it is immense, the entire domain of signification. For others, using a more restricted view, it is the study of non-linguistic communication: ritual, ceremonial codes, signal codes, and codes of polite behaviour, what we here designate, roughly, as technical or logical codes.

Still others include in semiology aesthetic or poetic codes: arts and literature, socialized behaviour (the art of social life). Hermeneutics may or may not be included. But how can the limits between these different types of signification be defined?

Everything is a sign, a luxuriant sprouting of signs; trees, clouds, faces, coffee-mills . . . are enamelled with layers of interpretation which twist and knead the semantic dough.

Everyone is more or less in agreement on the existence of this process of signifying, and the nature of the elements on which it is based. But in the perspective of a generalized semiotics, the different types of sign are 'more or less significant' so that it often becomes difficult to make out the limits of their field. In fact, it is possible to oppose, on the one hand, explicit, socialized codes in which the meaning is a datum of the message as a result of a formal convention between participants, and, on the other, the individual and more or less implicit hermeneutics in which meaning is the result of an interpretation on the part of the receiver. But it is far more difficult to define the precise nature of mixed systems, such as poetics, rhetorics, mantics, symbolics, or mythologies, some of which are hermeneutics undergoing codification, others of which are codes going through a process of decodification.

3

Logical codes

In the preceding pages, a distinction has been made between two major modes of experience: objective/intellective and subjective/affective.

The function of technical logical codes is to signify objective experience and the relation of man to the world. Several types can be distinguished: codes of knowledge in the double guise of scientific and traditional knowledge; signal systems, work and learning programmes which are action codes; and, finally, one may add here, for lack of a better place, the paralinguistic codes which are relays, substitutes and auxiliaries for articulated language.

1 Paralinguistic codes

As we have just seen, there are three types of paralinguistic code according to whether it is a question of simple recording, of an autonomous code, or of a parallel code used concurrently with language.

(1) THE RELAYS OF LANGUAGE

Under this heading we include the various *alphabets*, such as *written alphabets* (and as a possible category *syllabic* alphabets), *morse, braille, naval-style hand-operated flag systems*, the *deaf and dumb systems* and various kinds of *drum-beat* systems, one of the most rudimentary of which is the prisoners' alphabet: one tap for A, two taps for B, three taps for C, etc. This is the category to which *cryptographic* codes belong: they replace the letters of the alphabet by various sorts of figures, or they replace the normal order of the letters by means of specified rules (see Figure 4). Their function is to replace articulated language wherever the use of the latter is precluded for reasons of time or space. Hence sound is transposed into letters, and letters can be transformed into a totally different and yet appropriate substance. Writing transmutes sound into spatialized visual signs which enable the sounds to be preserved in time and transmitted through space. The digital deaf and dumb alphabet is visual, braille tactile. Morse can be acoustic, optical, written or electric.

One and the same message can be given several successive codings; an oral message is written down, then the ordinary written form is transformed into cryptographic code, and then into morse—the latter being first tactile (the movement of a knob), then recoded into electrical impulses, which are then put on to paper in the form of dots and dashes.

In all cases, such substitute codes have a phase of articulated language. That is why, despite their universality, they are comprehensible only in the recoded terms of articulated language.

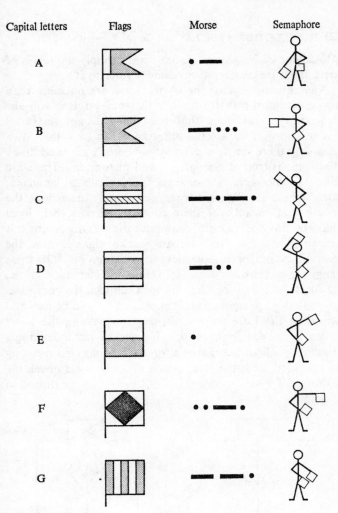

FIGURE 4

(2) THE SUBSTITUTES FOR LANGUAGE

Alphabetic codes are, as we have seen, simply the relays of articulated language and necessarily refer to it.

The alphabet's A or the · – in morse are no more than straightforward transcriptions of the sound *a*. It is only the substance of the code that has changed, not its form. Chinese ideograms, on the other hand, do have their own meaning; there are signs designating 'house', 'sky' and 'tree'. The same is true of hieroglyphs and pictograms. These are all autonomous codes, independent of articulated language; the Chinese intelligentsia can correspond throughout the length and breadth of their country whereas their local dialects do not permit communication. Others in this category are the Red Indian smoke signals, and the passwords of secret societies, and slang, etc. Of these language substitutes, one of the most elaborate is the gestural language of the Trappist monks. It comprises more than 1300 signs; *hour* is expressed by joining fists and waggling the little fingers; *evening* by pressing the index finger to the eye; *night* by pressing thumb and index finger on the eyes. Translation into a foreign language is a recoding of this kind, as is the film version of a play or a novel, the painting of a tale or battle, or conversely the description of a painting.

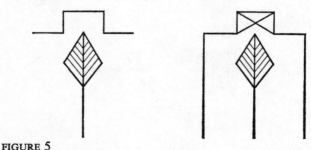

FIGURE 5

Figure 5, for example, shows a pictographic message. It is a love letter written by a girl of the Siberian Youkaghir tribe. The right-hand arrow represents the young girl, the left-hand arrow her fiancé. The lines enclosing the arrow represent a house. Only the roof of her fiancé's house is visible; this indicates that he is far away. The crossed beams on the girl's house indicate her sadness (reproduced from *L'Homme et son langage*, Tallandier, p. 109).

(3) THE AUXILIARIES OF LANGUAGE

Linguistic communication is based on the use of articulated signs. But discourse is often accompanied by other parallel sign systems: intonation, mimicry, gesture. These are natural, spontaneous indications, whose function is purely expressive, although some can be conventionalized for the purposes of communication. Shrugging the shoulders, raising the eyebrow, nodding or shaking one's head are signs which vary from culture to culture—for the Greeks, for example, 'nodding' the head from below upwards was a sign of negation.

These codes may be very elaborate in certain cultures: the Italian 'speaking with his hands' is not gesticulating vaguely as might be thought: every gesture has its own meaning. Such auxiliary systems play an important part in *theatre*, *dance* and *ritual* and their function is more expressive than technical (see below, p. 66).

(a) Codes of prosody utilize variations of pitch, quantity and intensity of articulated speech. Until now, semiology has abandoned these codes to linguistics, but the latter has never really studied them. The mistake has been to regard them as more or less marginal elements of the predicative grammatical code, sometimes studied under the name of suprasegmental signs. In fact, it is a parallel code closely

dovetailed into the predicative code but quite distinct both in terms of its function and its semiological role. Nothing demonstrates this more eloquently than the failure of grammar to account for and integrate such prosodic characteristics as interjection, imperative or vocative.

But the decisive criterion is the fact that language has a double level of articulation (cf. above, p. 32), which is not the case where prosodic signs are concerned.

The prosodic code plays an important part in affective communication and these originally natural indications are actually highly socialized and conventionalized, as is demonstrated in actors' diction.

(b) The kinesic code utilizes gestures and mimicry. Here again it is a case of a parallel code which is closely associated with speech and specially with prosodic signs.

The conventional character of these apparently spontaneous natural signs was demonstrated a long time ago. They have recently been the object of a scientific study in the USA. The problem will be taken up again in the context of the codes of social communication in which 'gestural languages play a particularly important part' (cf. below, p. 83).

(c) The proxemic code uses the space between emitter and receiver. The distance which we maintain between us and our interlocutor, the place we occupy in a procession or round a table, etc. are signs of our social status and constitute an elaborate code which varies from culture to culture. Like *kinesics*, proxemics constitutes a science newly born in the USA and to which we shall return.[1]

---

[1] For these matters 'Pratiques et langages gestuels', *Langages*, no. 10, June 1968 (Didier-Larousse) can usefully be consulted. It contains a discussion of these problems and a bibliography.

2 Practical codes: signals and programmes

The function of *signals* and *programmes* is to co-ordinate action by means of injunctions, instructions, notices or warnings. Groups use signals to co-ordinate their movements. Programmes are systems of instructions used to carry out a task, e.g. the programme used on an assembly line or by the boss of a fashion house.

The highway code, the railway, air space, marine or river codes are among the best-known signal systems. Warning signals such as bells and alarms, drum beats, gongs, horns and sirens can be elaborate. Thus, the military reveille, alarm call, call to horse, the retreat and the charge may even have variations according to the different military corps or units.

All forms of communal work use signals: from the yo-heave-ho of the sailors hauling a main-sheet to the most complex programmes of an assembly line or of a battle order.

Some are very simple, e.g. the blind man's white stick; others are very complicated, e.g. the highway code which comprises several hundred signs of the most diverse substance and form: lights, colours, images, letters, auditory signals, etc.

The nature of these systems depends, on the one hand, on which semiological field they belong to; that is to say on the information and orders which they are called upon to transmit; and, on the other hand, it depends upon the conditions of emission and reception. How, for example, can a baled-out pilot communicate with planes flying over the place where the accident occurred? Hailing is out of the question, gestures and flags are indistinct beyond a certain distance, flares are not efficient in daylight. The matter is solved by using a square of material which is blue on one side and yellow on the other and which can therefore be folded according to a code which has twelve signs that correspond to requests for water, food, medical supplies, fuel, etc.

It is not possible here to make an inventory of all those systems. Here, as a sample, however, are a few remarks on the *highway code*. This is particularly important in so far as it is of interest to the majority of citizens with respect to no inconsiderable part of their activities. G. Mounin has calculated that the highway code in France uses almost 150 different signals (not to mention the 230 bits of information carried by foreign and national automobile registration plates). These are: 87 road sign panels belonging to five different semantic categories: danger, stop, prohibition, obligation, parking; 25 to 30 light signals: red, green, amber, trafficators, brake lights, reversing lights, filter arrows, parking lights, night position, exceptionally large convoys; about 20 types of traffic lines: pedestrian crossings, continuous or broken yellow lines, red or yellow curb marks relating to parking or loading; and 5 signs concerning the nature of the vehicle; not counting the stationary or moving arm signals of the police.

G. Mounin has shown, furthermore ('Les systèmes de communication non-linguistiques', *BSLP*, 44, 1959) that:

> A motorist registers an average of 200–250 signs per 100 km in the direction he is travelling on a national highway; up to 500 signals per 100 km if passing through towns is included; and town traffic alone uses between 800 and 1000 signs per 100 km, counting only highway code signs, which are by no means the only traffic signs.

Signal systems vary according to their complexity, to their degree of structuration, and the nature of the signs used. Some are arbitrary, e.g. road or maritime light signals; others are iconographic, e.g. the panels indicating the proximity of a school, of a level-crossing, etc.

They have one thing in common, however: their strictly monosemic character, a high degree of convention which is always explicit and constraining. And today most are international.

Signals are of all kinds: we have already mentioned alarms, bells and drum rolls. To these could be added, war cries (and sporting cries), smoke signals, beacons, the hunters' tree-markings, the beggars' code, the code of the criminal underworld: these are so many means of transmitting instructions with a view to collective or individual action.

In the case of complex, elaborate action, the signal takes the form of a programme. A programme is:

> An ordered formalized set of operations which are necessary and sufficient to obtain a particular result; a device which enables a mechanism to carry out these operations; perforated tape, magnetic tape programmes, calculator or computer programmes.

These definitions, given in one of the most recent French dictionaries, illustrate the importance which the term 'programme' has taken on with automation. But cybernetics is a discipline which we have chosen to ignore, although it could easily take its place within the framework of a semiology. In computer programming the programme is often diagrammatic: a construction plan, an assembly diagram, flow charts, etc. (cf. *La Cybernétique*, 'Que sais-je?' series, no. 688, PUF).

3 Epistemological codes

Insignia and signals are signs of communication; their explicit function is to convey information concerning the identity of individuals or groups and to transmit information necessary for the co-ordination of an action.

In a different way, signs can function as representatives of a complex reality and indicators of the structure of such reality. In fact, all knowledge consists of the establishment of a system of relations between the elements which constitute the field of an experience; and once these relations have been observed or postulated, they must be signified.

So there are two sides to the coin of knowledge: an epistemological system (signified) and a semiological system (signifying). The aim of semiology is to establish the nature of the relation between these two systems. In modern science these relations are characteristically signified by means of an *ad hoc* system of signifiers which is specially conceived for this purpose in conformity with an objectivist system of axioms. Traditional knowledge, on the other hand, borrows pragmatic models from already known and coded reality. The 'new' epistemological system is represented by means of another *episteme* which is, or is assumed to be, of analogous form.

There are innumerable systems of these two kinds. Here, by way of example, we shall limit ourselves to the brief description of a few scientific codes and some mantic codes which constitute the most typical forms of systematic knowledge in 'primitive' cultures.

SCIENTIFIC CODES

Each science and system of knowledge has its special language based on its own specific mode of signification, but ordinary language acts as a matrix and mother-tongue for them all. My *Mots savants* ('Que sais-je?' series, no. 1325, PUF) can usefully be consulted in this connection.

But these scientific languages, whatever the degree of their autonomy, are, by virtue of their relation to language in general, subject to all kinds of contamination (polysemia, analogy, connotations, etc.), which distort their nature and interfere with their functioning. This is why most sciences attempt to elaborate non-linguistic codes which are particularly appropriate to their own individual axiomatic structure.

These codes are logical, as opposed to aesthetic (see above, p. 10), because the aim of all science is to concentrate on referential functions and to minimize any interference or connotation that may arise from any other functions: emotive, injunctional, etc.

The two major categories of signification found in scientific codes are (1) arbitrary and (2) diagrammatic. Numerical notation is entirely arbitrary, but geometry uses diagrams. Algebraic functions can be represented both by arbitrary formulae and by diagrams. Plans, schemata and graphs are figurative. But all these codes have in common the fact that they are highly conventionalized, restrictive and generally explicit.

The dual prerequisite of a scientific code is that it should be (1) arbitrary so as to avoid any analogical contamination, and (2) a type of motivation which facilitates the task of memory. This is why they are generally structured in homological fashion. Such is the case of the language of chemistry, in which there is perfect correspondence between the structure of signifiers and that of the signifieds, but there is no analogy between the elements of the two series.

Scientific codes are divided according to two major functions: classification and calculation; hence the two main categories: taxonomic and algorithmic (or operational).

The taxonomies of the natural sciences (flora, fauna, etc.) are purely classificatory systems whose function is to define entities in terms of their reciprocal relations. On the other hand, algebraic formulae enable one to transform the relations which they express into new relations.

Amongst the sciences one can distinguish those which study pure abstract relations which are independent of their content, and those which, on the contrary, study the relations among their contents. In this perspective, the most abstract of all sciences is *logic*: it is the study of relations as such, and is thus the science of science.. Its aim is to define the various types of relations which can obtain among entities or sets, and to guarantee the truth of these relations. To the extent that logic signifies these relations it is a code. That of traditional (Aristotelian) logic is constituted by a body of syllogisms. Modern formal logic has acquired a set of entirely arbitrary and systematized signs. Modern formal logic is also called symbolic logic, where symbolic is used in the logical sense of the word, and one which we avoid for reasons already set out (cf. above, p. 23).

Mathematics is the study of relations which are specified, but independently of substance and at a very high level of abstraction. *Arithmetic* and *algebra* deal with numerical relations, *geometry* with spatial, and *mechanics* with kinetic relations.

Physics and *chemistry* study relations of substance. All these sciences have ideogrammatical notation systems which have the additional advantage of being international. As Mounin explains ('Les systèmes de communication non-linguistiques', p. 186):

> The best known of these systems is none other than the table of standard abbreviations of the metric system, which boasts no less than 67 universal symbols (of arithmetic, of length, breadth, width, volume, fluid measure and weight).
> The system of physical units (MTS, CGS, MKSA) in turn contains at least 285 universal symbols which express either units (175 of them); size (110) corresponding to each and every sector of each aspect of physics: mass, time, mechanics, electricity, magnetism, heat, optics (in all 37 sections

each with different concepts and their corresponding units expressed in symbols which stand for the following: hertz, sthene, newton, dyne, joule, erg, watt, bar, pieze, pascal, barye, ampere, volt, ohm, coulomb, farad, henry, weber, maxwell, gauss, therm, calorie, frigorie, candela, nit, stilb, lumen, candle, phot, lux, dioptre, var). Contemporary chemistry offers an even more highly conventionalized vocabulary of thousands of symbols which combine according to rigorous, systematic laws (which are the ideographic expression of the objective laws of chemistry).

To this must be added the fact that these sciences possess figurative codes: algebraic functions, statistical curves, chemical configurations, etc. Here, for example, is how the primrose is described in the botanical code: the formula for the plant is:

$$\ddot{\varphi} \oplus K(5) \; \overparen{C(5) \; AO} + 5G(5)$$

which reads: 'Hermaphrodite, radial symmetry, five-sepalled calyx, five-petalled corolla with five attached stamens, and a five-carpelled pistil the ovaries of which are placed higher than the level at which the petals are inserted.'

In similar vein, zoology describes a jaw as follows:

$$\frac{I_3 \quad C_1 \quad P_4 \quad M_3}{I_3 \quad C_1 \quad P_4 \quad M_3} = 44$$

which means that lower and upper jaw are identical and are composed, respectively, of 3 incisors, 1 canine, 4 premolars and 3 molars, making 44 teeth in all.

Now, here is the formula for a chemical experiment:

$$CaCo_3 + H_2SO_4 = CaSO_4 + CO_2 + H_2O$$

which means that if calcium carbonate (marble) and sulphuric acid are mixed, one obtains calcium sulphate, carbon dioxide gas and water.

The *chemical equation* is of the same nature as an algebraic equation and can be verified in the same way: the sum of the units is the same in the two terms but their combinations are different.

All these codes are articulated and structured, and their meaning depends upon the homology between their epistemological and their semiological systems.

These transcription codes are paralleled by graphic representation, such as the graphs of algebraic functions, taxonomic trees, and molecular models of physics and chemistry.

The signs are arbitrary and leave no room for any substantive analogy between signified and signifier. This is true both of transcription codes and representational systems.

The coding of traditional knowledge, however, is based on systems where the signifier is an analogue of the signified. In their scholarly and elaborated forms, astrology, alchemy, physiognomy, etc. are exhaustive systems which, in general, use homological modes of signification. But, whereas science creates *ad hoc* sign systems in a way which is entirely arbitrary and which reflects only the epistemological system, traditional knowledge seeks a signification system within another real concrete epistemological system. Thus the soul and its functions are assimilated to the body, social organization to celestial structure, etc.

Now, such assimilation, even where its principle is purely formal and structural, leads to analogical association between the entities of the two systems. There is a transfer of substantive properties from the signifier to the signified. Thus in a system in which the *soul* (*anima*) is designated by 'breath', bad breath becomes a sign of corruption of the soul.

Such systems of prelogical signification can be called homo-analogical. This is also a characteristic of the 'savage mind' (*la pensée sauvage*) in Lévi-Strauss's expression, a general rule of the creation myth and folklore. The mechanism is fairly obvious in the divinatory codes which form the basis of knowledge in primitive cultures, and which survive in our own contemporary popular thinking.

4 The 'savage mind': mantic codes

Mantic codes constitute the art of divination and the means of communicating with the gods, the beyond, or destiny. They are sign systems.

In the West, the best-known are divination by means of the stars (*astrology*), by means of cards (*cartomancy*), lines of the palm (*palmistry*), and dreams (*oneiromancy*); not to mention coffee grounds, crystal gazing, etc. There are innumerable varieties.

The *Encyclopédie de la divination* (Tchou, Paris, 1965) enumerates 350, a list which is no doubt far from exhaustive, and to which should be added innumerable superstitions.

The sign may be isolated: *a black cat, red sky at night, red in the morning*, etc., but the message may also be formulated in terms of a complex combination of signs organized according to a code.

Here, for example, is one of the vast numbers of ways of telling the cards. Out of a pack of 52 cards 20 are drawn and dealt into five piles of four cards placed in the form of a cross. The cards in the middle tell of the present; those above, of the near future; those below of the past; those on the right, of the distant future; those on the left, of obstacles.

Each pile of four cards constitutes a message which must be interpreted as a whole, taking into account the proximity relations between the cards, each of which has a conventional meaning. Hearts and clubs are favourable, diamonds and spades unfavourable. Hearts mean love and success; clubs mean friendship and money. Diamonds: infidelity or journeys and news. Spades: jealousy and failure. The *king, queen* and *knave* represent a man, a woman and a young man respectively.

The *king of hearts* is a 'bosom friend'.

The *king of clubs* is a 'faithful friend'.

The *king of diamonds* is an 'insolent stranger'.

The *king of spades* is a 'brutal, avaricious husband'.

The *knave of diamonds* is a 'flattering and interested young stranger'.

The *seven* designates a girl, the *seven of diamonds* represents 'an unknown girl, misfortune in love', etc.

The fortune-teller, having learnt that her lady client is at present engaged in an adventure with a young man (centre pile), perceives obstacles (left-hand pile) in the form of the rivalry of a scheming lady (queen of diamonds) or a brutal father (king of spades), and foresees in the immediate future (top pile) reverses such as separation (nine of spades) or a journey (ten of diamonds); the distant future (right-hand pile) may hold a successful outcome (nine of hearts), thanks to the actions of a faithful friend (queen or knave of diamonds).

Each of these combinations allows for great latitude in interpretation, thus enabling previous information to be integrated; the *king of spades* may be a husband, father, jealous lover, etc., the *ten of diamonds* (journey) may be a transitory or final departure, the journey of two people together, the appearance of a traveller, an encounter during a journey, etc.

These systems are most instructive for the semiologist in so far as they inform us about the function and functioning of cultural codes (cf. above, p. 58). They constitute a grid applied to a situation in the above instance, the classical naïve love affair; but it can also be applied to war, politics, business, etc., so that the same message can be read in as many ways as one wishes.

Such readings are all homologous to the extent that it is

the same system of relations between signifiers which is imposed on them. And, reciprocally, different grids, astrological or oneiric, can be applied to the same reality.

Thus, there are systems of relations, each with its own structure: cards, stars, dreams, etc., and each of these structures, when applied to reality, carves it up into analogous relations and in so doing confers upon it a certain meaning, the meaning being nothing other than a relation (cf. below, p. 63).

The code is an assimilation of the unknown to the known which lends the unknown the structure (and hence the meaning) of the known. Astrology postulates that the relations among men are homologous with those observed among stars, both in space (celestial configurations) and in time (movement of the stars). The physiognomic systems rest on the similar postulate of an equivalence between the body (visible) and the soul (invisible): intelligence and the head go together; feelings go with the heart; will and instincts with the belly; and action with sex. As for dreams, they use a cultural symbolism which psychoanalysis justifies in terms of archetypes of the imagination and messages of the subconscious.

All cultures have their symbol systems. Table 3 shows some of those of Western dream-based fortune-telling.

This symbolism is often shared by different fortune-telling techniques: ink-blots, sand, clouds, coffee grounds; in any of these a ring is an augury of marriage, etc. The systems which we have just mentioned are classed as motivated because they use real structures (stars, cards, the lines on one's hands).

Other techniques of divination are quite arbitrary in the sense that the code is an abstract construct, and the signs are purely logical (and not natural) combinations. Such are *arithmomancy* (divination by numbers), *paromancy* (divination by means of small rods), and various types of spell.

TABLE 3

Lamb:	tranquillity, happiness
Eagle:	fire, devastation
Needle:	difficulty, danger
Donkey:	sensuality, love affairs, adultery
Angel:	good news
Ring:	marriage or divorce (according to context), or prison
Spider:	good omen

All cultures, but especially the Egyptians, Hebrews, Greeks and Arabs, used *arithmomantic* calculations. They survive in innumerable forms, one of the most naïve of which is interpreting one's character and future in terms of one's name. To this end, each letter is numbered from its order in the alphabet, e.g. P.I.E.R.R.E. becomes $16+9+5+18+18+5 = 71 = 8$. Next it is simply a matter of interpreting the figure 8 in terms of a code, and there are many codes. Some work back to the symbolism which stems from the ancient arithmology, others are tables of equivalence between the integers and the planets, in which case the arithmomantic code is merely a mediation for astrology.

Of all these systems one of the most complete and most logically and abstractly structured is the Chinese *I Ching* or divination by means of little rods. These, according to whether they are even or odd, supply two sign elements, and each sign or hexagram is composed of six elements. There are 64 hexagrams in the code and each has a well-defined meaning.

Divination is the set of responses which the client expects from the fortune-teller in any given situation: war, family, health, love, business. There is a sign for each element and the signs are drawn by chance. The hand that draws the rods or the cords, traces in the sand or ashes, or the animal that leaves its spoor is supposed to be guided by destiny. What the fortune-teller does is to make sense of the individual objects and of the phenomena that the client consults him or her about; that is to establish relations between them. This is the aim of all knowledge. Science establishes objective and really existent relations amongst things; divination projects its own structure on to the universe. Nevertheless, in certain cases there may be a real homology between the structure of the code and that of reality.

Psychoanalysis has confirmed the value of numerous symbols, and views dreams as veritable communications from the unconscious. Psychosomatic medicine today accepts that disease may be a mode of communication and, in particular, that it may reflect disturbances or absence of the ability to communicate normally. The palmist—by insight or by tradition—sometimes comes to conclusions which are not without some basis in reality: the colour of the hand, the tone of the muscles, the width of the wrist, etc. Thus, making a fist in such a way that the thumb is enclosed by the fingers has been recognized by medicine as a sign of lack of will-power observable in timid or mal-adjusted people, as well as in serious pathological states. This has been confirmed by psychoanalysis, which sees in it the sign of a 'nostalgia for foetal bliss'.

But 'primitive thought' or 'the savage mind' (*la pensée sauvage*) postulates an unverified analogy between two distinct series of phenomena; this, as we have said, is a homo-analogy, whereas science is founded on a system of axioms which it derives from observation of the phenomena considered in themselves. Table 4 shows correspondences between the signs of the Zodiac, the hand, the body and diseases, tarots, numbers, letters, etc. Other correspondences involve numbers, the letters of the alphabet, etc.

Ancient medical knowledge is based on this system, from which it derives a diagnostic method and a pharmacopoeia inherited by numerous horoscope systems. Thus on 23 April

TABLE 4

Zodiac	Tarot	Geomancy	Human body	Colours	Precious stones	Metals	Fingers	
Aries	The Emperor	Acquisitio	Head, Face	Red	Amethyst	Steel	Index	1
Taurus	The Pope	Laetitia	Neck, Throat	Green	Agate	Brass	—	2
Gemini	The Lover	Rubens	Arm	Grey	Beryl	Mercury	—	3
Cancer	The Chariot	Albus	Breast	Blue	Emerald	Silver	Ring	1
Leo	The Force	Via	Back, Heart	Yellow	Ruby	Gold	—	2
Virgo	The Hermit	Conjunctio	Belly	Grey	Jasper	Nickel-silver	—	3
Libra	Justice	Puer	Loins, Small of the back	Green	Diamond	Copper	Little	1
Scorpio	Death	Tristitia	Sexual organs	Red	Topaz	Iron	—	2
Sagittarius	Temperance	Cauda Draconis	Buttocks, Thighs	Blue	Garnet	Tin	—	3
Capricorn	The Devil	Populus	Liver	Black	Onyx	Lead	Middle	1
Aquarius	The Star	Fortuna	Calves, Ankles	?	Sapphire	Nickel	—	2
Pisces	The Moon	Carcer	Feet, Toes	Blue	Chrysolite	Zinc	—	3

1970 *Jours de France* advises Virgo: 'You have exhausted your body by too rich a diet. Take care of it by eating fresh vegetables, light meals, fresh cream, fresh-water fish, unsalted butter.' This is because the sign of Virgo corresponds to the belly and intestines, and its illness is dropsy. Sagittarius, which corresponds to the liver, is advised: 'Go easy on your liver,' etc. In a similar way the whole of alchemy is dependent on astrology; the various metals each have a sign the horoscope of which is cast by the alchemist so as to facilitate the conjunctions. In this connection the works of Bachelard can usefully be consulted, in particular his *La Formation de l'esprit scientifique. Contribution à une psychanalyse de la connaissance objective* (Vrin, 1972, 8th edition).

It is obviously not an accident that astrology serves as a homo-analogical code for other studies, because, of all the phenomena of nature, it constitutes the most rigorous and the most stable numerical, spatial and temporal system. Alchemy, medicine, physiognomy, psychology all borrowed from astrology just as today linguistics, economics and sociology seek their models in mathematics.

This polyvalence of codes is at the origin of the *hermeneutic* systems of interpretation and decoding. But, whereas the code of a message is explicitly given by the sender, a hermeneutics is a grid supplied by the receiver: a philosophical, aesthetic, or cultural grid which he applies to the text.

Homo-analogical codes are capable of being interpreted in this way. So are systems which, either by their nature or as a result of a history of demotivation and disintegration, are weakly codified. Such, in particular, is the case where aesthetic or cultural codes are concerned. This is why literary criticism and anthropology remain essentially hermeneutic even if they deny it by attempting to justify their systems as unconscious codes.

4

Aesthetic codes

We have emphasized the fundamental distinction between two antithetical modes of experience and two corresponding types of semiological code: logical experience and affective or aesthetic experience.

The former concerns the objective perception of the external world, the elements of which are enclosed rationally in a system of relations. The latter involves the subjective impressions which reality makes upon the human spirit.

The term *aesthetic* is justified here by virtue of the fact that this mode of expression is characteristic of the arts and literature. But in a wider sense, too, it is justified by the etymology of the word which, in Greek, designates the 'faculty of feeling', derived from the adjective *aisthêtos*, which means 'perceptible to the senses'. The term *aesthetic* does not therefore apply here simply to the 'beautiful' but also to the concrete, the sensible—an etymological force which Valéry revived when he forged the neologism *esthésique*.

In its pure state the logical sign is arbitrary and homological to the extent that it signifies form but not substance (in the sense of the terms current in linguistics since Hjelmslev). The aesthetic sign is iconic and analogical. The arts are modes of representation of reality, and aesthetic signifiers are perceptible objects. To speak of 'abstract painting' is erroneous because all painting is concrete; as for 'non-figurative painting', at the level of the signifier it merits the name, but the visual signifier is a representation and an icon of that non-figurative reality. This is why the aesthetic message does not have a simple transitive function which leads to meaning; it is of value in itself; it is an object, a message-object.

This hypostasis of the aesthetic signifier constitutes the fundamental character of what R. Jakobson has defined as the 'poetic function' (cf. above, p. 7). Art is subjective, it *affects* the subject, that is to say, it 'touches the human organism or psyche by means of an impression or action'; whereas science is objective, it structures the object.

Science signifies an order imposed upon nature; art, an emotion which we experience *vis-à-vis* nature. That is why aesthetic signs are images of reality. Science is transitive (in the grammatical sense of the word), and art intransitive. With the help of science we signify the world by enclosing it within the network of reason; art enables us to signify ourselves by deciphering our psyche in terms of the order of nature.

By virtue of their iconic character aesthetic signs are far less conventionalized and thus far less codified and socialized than logical signs (see above, p. 24). To be sure, they *are* conventional, some are even highly conventionalized; but convention never imposes upon them (as happens with logical signs) the constraints of necessity and generality. Taking the extreme case, the aesthetic sign is free from all convention and its meaning adheres to representation. This property confers upon it a creative power; poetry is a 'making' (a *poiésie* was Valéry's neologism). The 'maker' (*poiète*)—like the troubadour—is an 'inventor' of signs: of signs in the making, relational expressions in the process of formulation, nascent or spontaneous signs which achieve their veritable semiological status only to the extent that they are generalized and that their signifying relation becomes explicit.

Such a definition would seem to exclude the arts from the domain of semiology to the extent that by definition all signs are conventional and socialized. But, as previously mentioned, there are degrees of conventionality and degrees of socialization (cf. p. 41, above). These characteristics are no more than ideal types, and from this perspective two types of aesthetic signs and messages can be distinguished: *rhetoric* and *poetic*. Rhetorics and styles of writing are conventional systems; as for *poetic* signs, they have been retrieved today by new postulates and new methods of analysis.

The decisive factors, in this connection, were the impact of psychoanalysis and the notion of an individual and collective unconscious. 'Deep' analysis shows that even apparently vague and labile signs are rooted in coherent structures, underlying codes from which they obtain their values.

Furthermore, it appears that these aesthetic systems assume a double function. Some are representatives of the unknown, beyond the realm of logical codes; means of apprehending the Invisible, the Ineffable, the Irrational and, in general, abstract psychic experience through the concrete experience of the senses. Others signify our desires by re-creating imaginary—archaic or futurist—worlds or societies to compensate for the defects and frustrations of the world and society as experienced. The former are ways of obtaining knowledge even if it is knowledge of the unknown; the latter are *divertimenti* in the etymological sense of the term.

1 Arts and literature

The arts are representations of nature and of society, real or imaginary, visible or invisible, objective or subjective. The arts utilize the media and their corresponding codes; but starting with that primary signification they create signified structures which themselves are signifying. The same is true of literature; it is a language-based art and creates signifying linguistic objects.

Myths are literary forms: *muthos*, in Greek, means 'narrative', and this is also the meaning of 'legend' from the Latin *legenda*, which means 'destined to be read'. Myths, legends, and popular or folk literature, in general, are of the greatest interest for semiology in so far as they express archaic, simple and universal situations. It is here that there is a real chance of unearthing clear, coherent structures. The practitioners of semiology have made no mistake about this, and have so far tackled the *structure* of the folk tale, the western, the detective story, the comic strip, etc. This semiological approach has its origins in the work of the Russian formalists, who, from the 1920s on, conceived of literary criticism as a structural study of content. Little known outside Russia, where it was, moreover, soon to die out, formalism was taken up by students of linguistics of the Prague School, who busied themselves with content in relation to the various genres. As a parallel development, there evolved a study of literary themes and their symbolic meaning considered as systems of structured signs.

The two disciplines taking their cue from other human sciences, anthropology and sociology, borrowed their methodology and their epistemological code from linguistics. This semiological study of literature is today in full swing with Anglo-Saxon New Criticism, Germanic *Literaturwissenschaft*, and the French *Nouvelle Critique*. The latter has so far operated in two domains: the form of morphology of narrative, and the study of symbolic archetypes.

2 Symbolism and thematics

The study of primitive religion has long ago demonstrated the symbolic character of ritual, myth, art and literature. These are representations of the world in which numbers, elementary forms (the circle, square, spiral, etc.), animals and plants are signs. On these matters we refer the reader to *La Symbolique* (Que sais-je?' series, no. 749, PUF) and to the works of Mircea Eliade and G. Dumézil.

Here, as an example, is an interpretation of the *Temple of the Sky* in Peking given by Beigbeder in *La Symbolique* (Paris, pp. 45–50):

> We have observed the coexistence in China of the notions of the Mountain, the Pillar of the Sky, of the infernal abyss and the celestial circle; and we have referred to the importance of natural open-air sanctuaries such as the *Temple of the Sky* in Peking or the *Sacrificial Area* of Hué. Let us now examine how these notions are harmonized in these sanctuaries. The subtlety of the Chinese is always haunted by binary division, and in these temples there is an opposition between the square, symbolizing the earth, and the circle symbolizing the heavens. In the *Temple of the Sky* one can distinguish two parts which are united by a south-north alley. To the south the sacrificial area is a spherical mound surrounded by a square precinct; the mound has three storeys each of which one reaches by a flight of three steps at the four points of the compass. The base of the mound is composed of 9×9 flagstones —figures which allude to the nine levels of the Chinese heaven. The sacrifices to the gods take place on a pyre

from which the smoke goes up to the sky, and blood
of the sacrificial animal flows through a hole down to
the earth. To the north, the round pavilion, seat of the
god, is borne by eight pillars—eight for the points of
the compass and for the 'moorings of the earth'.

The temple is thus a representation of the world, and it
utilizes a sign system which is found in the majority of
cultures, e.g. the pyramid or cosmic mountain turns up in
Mesopotamia and Egypt as well as in pre-Columbian
cultures.

These symbols can be shown to penetrate the cultural
field as a whole: costume, habitat, games, etc. Thus,
according to Beigbeder,

> the *pelota* type game of the Mayan civilization, and the
> *curved stick game* [lacrosse] of the Fox Indians (in the
> Great Lakes area) have a profound cosmological
> meaning. The Fox Indians' game is played on a circular
> terrain which is divided into two parts, Earth and Sky;
> the two teams symbolize the living and the dead; other
> lunar symbolic associations link the Earth to the night,
> to the moon, to the maternal springtime, to the south,
> to the left-hand side, to physical well-being and to
> material necessity; and other links unite the Sky with
> day, the sun, the paternal principle, the right-hand
> side, ritual and the creation of the world.

This exemplifies a particularly well-structured and coherent code. And modern psychoanalysis has shown that
these codes survive, in latent form, in the unconscious. In
this connection the fundamental work to be consulted is
C. G. Jung, *The Metamorphosis of the Soul and its Symbols*.
Here is a sample:

> An intelligent patient who is well aware of the
> roundness of the earth and its rotation round the sun,

replaces, in his paranoid system, modern astronomic knowledge by a minutely detailed system in which the earth is a flat disc above which the sun moves.

Dr Spielrein gives similar interesting examples of archaic definitions which in illness replace the contemporary meaning of words. Thus, for example, one of her patients presents a mythological analogy for alcohol and intoxicating beverages by speaking of 'ejaculation' (in other words: Soma). She also has a cooking symbol-structure which is analogous to the alchemical vision of Zosimos. The latter saw, in the hollow of the altar, boiling water in which men underwent metamorphosis. The patient used *earth* or water in place of *mother*.

As the author points out, these are archetypes of the imagination which are found in all cultures in the most diverse forms. It is evident that they survive in modern art.

Gaston Bachelard has shown the existence of these profound themes of poetic imagination by establishing the meanings and connotations of the images of Earth, Water, Fire and Air. There is a comparable symbolic system built round space, the human body, etc. The deepest poetic experience, often unconscious and ineffable, is expressed by means of cultural codes (with individual variants) which are systems of structured signs comparable to those found in myths, rituals and divinatory procedures. To be sure, literary criticism has from the very beginning been concerned with the study of themes (Nature, Love, Death, etc.) and the imagery of the great writers. But below what until recently were thought of as isolated signs we today recognize the existence of systems of opposition from which the signs draw their meaning. It is to the reconstruction of these underlying systems that contemporary criticism turns its attention, borrowing its models and definitions from linguistics.

We take the liberty of referring the reader to our *Essais de stylistique* (Paris, Klinsksieck, 1970) in which are to be found the description of a certain number of these *stylistic fields*: Baudelaire's abyss, Mallarmé's azure, Valéry's shadow.

Here, for example, is our reconstruction of the symbol-structure of the *Fleurs du Mal*:

The lexicon of the *Fleurs du Mal* comprises some four thousand words, which divide along four main lines of force which circumscribe the Baudelairean universe and constitute its material and spiritual setting: Heaven, Hell, Earth (this is twofold and is contrasted with Life, the day-to-day destiny of the poet in the city) and the Dream, which is a flight into the exotic. Life unfolds in the muddy streets of a dirty, noisy, vulgar, foggy, miserable city associated with impotence, infirmity, ugliness, poverty, prostitution, vice, physical and moral decadence. It is a place of boredom, spleen and suffering, a place of exile (cf. 'Le cygne', 'Les petites vieilles', etc.).

The Dream enables us to evade this sojourn where love is impossible; we escape to islands, perfumes, rhythms, harmony, idleness, luxury, vigour, health, youth and sensuous pleasures (cf. 'La chevelure', 'Parfum exotique', etc.). In this context, a youthful voyage to the islands is often invoked; its theme seems singularly conventional, schematized and stylized, as a compensation for a life of frustration, where all the negatives of the latter are located: the climate is hot and sunny because the city is foggy, muddy, rainy and icy; it is a land of perfumes because the streets are foul and the hovels filthy; it is a sojourn of peace and harmony because the city is vulgar, raucous and harassing; it is a land in which one soul loves another because here love is impossible, impotent, abject and vile, and lovers are separated, torn apart.

Apart from such exotic reverie, there is another kind of evasion into the artificial paradise of wine and debauch.

This horizontal universe has a vertical dimension: Hell and Heaven. In Hell crime, lust and madness crawl in the icy darkness and the dizziness of a nightmare. To this horror-filled abyss is opposed the azure limpid deep, brilliant, warm sky of Heaven, inhabited by liberty, purity, power, beauty and serenity. Analogous to the sky is the immense, deep eternal sea; mounting into the azure sky and cradling on the blue of the waves are the two major euphoric Baudelairean experiences. It is a dialectical vision in which the happiness of ascent is opposed to the terror of falling.

These two worlds are systematically antithetical, so that any one term naturally implies all its analogues and all its contraries. And this same dialectic also defines life 'in which action is not the sister of dream' and in which the sweetness of the dream remains forever opposed by a boring daily life which is rejected.

The whole of Baudelaire's *œuvre* fits into this poetic cosmogony, where *Here* is dominated by the expanse within these four cardinal points: the exotic dream, poetry and love under the dual influence of Heaven and the Abyss, debauchery and alcohol are as much ways of escape as a spleen-inducing and abhorrent here-and-now.

Each of these points constitutes a structured verbal space which is in correspondence with the others. The emblematic of Azure is opposed to that of the Abyss but shares its attributes with the Sea. Debauch is marked by all the signs of the fall, of vertigo, of nightmare and madness which are associated with the Abyss, while the artificial paradise of wine can for a brief instant capture the euphoria of Heaven.

Such is the map of the Journey which ends in the stillness of Death. The Baudelairean drama is set in this decor, the focal points of which would, in medieval theatre, have been referred to as so many 'mansions'. Four main categories of women participate in the drama of love: angels, demons, distant sisters, prostitutes. There is no place for love on earth; woman is venal, hideous, sordid; ephemeral embraces in a kind of annihilation, stupor, or vile debauch replace love (XXXIV):

> One night when I was close to a hideous Jewess
> Like a corpse stretched out along another corpse . . .

Lust is a pathetic attempt to accomplish an impossible union; union of bodies is evil and sin hurls the lovers into the abyss. Jeanne Duval typifies such demons (though the cycle in which she appears touches upon the other themes); she is a 'weird deity dark as night', 'an ebony-thighed witch', 'a pitiless demon', 'impure woman', 'a deaf, cruel soul', 'vampire', 'herd of demons'; such is the 'child of blackest midnight' with whom all his life long the poet plunges into the vertigo of furious and culpable love.

> O pitiless demon! Diminish your flames;
> I am not the Styx that I should embrace you
> nine times.
>
> ('Sed Non Satiata')

This hell is that of women damned.

> Go down, go down, pitiable victims,
> Go down the path to eternal hell.
> Plunge into the depth of the abyss where all the crimes
> Lashed by a wind that comes from above . . .

In conclusion, here is a definition of *archetype* given by Northrop Frye, one of the leading figures of the *New Criticism* (*Anatomy of Criticism*, pp. 102–3):

> Archetypes are associative clusters, and differ from signs in being complex variables. Within the complex is often a large number of specific learned associations which are communicable because a large number of

people in a given culture happen to be familiar with them. When we speak of 'symbolism' in ordinary life we usually think of such learned cultural archetypes as the cross or the crown, or of conventional associations, as of white with purity or green with jealousy. As an archetype, green may symbolize hope, or vegetable nature, or a go sign in traffic, or Irish patriotism as easily as jealousy, but the word green as a verbal sign always refers to a certain colour. Some archetypes are so deeply rooted in conventional association that they can hardly avoid suggesting that association, as the geometrical figure of the cross inevitably suggests the death of Christ.

A *completely* conventionalized art would be an art in which the archetypes, or communicable units, were essentially a set of esoteric signs. This can happen in the arts—for instance, in some of the sacred dances of India—but it has not happened in Western literature yet, and the resistance of modern writers to having their archetypes 'spotted', so to speak, is due to a natural anxiety to keep them as versatile as possible, not pinned down exclusively to one interpretation. A poet may be showing an esoteric tendency if he specifically points out one association, as Yeats does in his footnotes to some of his early poems.

These are not *necessary* associations; there are some exceedingly obvious ones, such as the association of darkness with terror or mystery, but there are no intrinsic or inherent correspondences which must invariably be present. As we shall see later, there is a context in which the phrase 'universal symbol' makes sense, but it is not this context. The stream of literature, like any other stream, seeks the easiest channels first: the poet who uses the expected associations will communicate more rapidly.

3 The morphology of narrative

We have just studied systems of signs in which the forms of the natural or human world are invested with analogical signification. These systems—symbolics—are systems of transcoding which signify an experience by means of another experience which thus imposes its own structure on the former.

The literary or aesthetic work includes characters, events and situations. It has always been known that these elements can be reduced to typical categories. In the theatre there are standard roles: the innocent, the traitor, the confidant, etc., and standard situations: love thwarted, punishment, vengeance.

But the originality of modern criticism is, once again, that it considers these facts as structured systems and borrows its models from linguistics. For example, Emile Souriau in *Les Deux cent mille situations dramatiques* shows that dramatic situations are constructed by combining six functions which correspond to six principal roles: the arbiter, the opponent, etc.

It was the Russian formalists who from the 1920s onwards posed the problem of the structure of the literary work. The classic work in this domain is V. Propp's *Morphology of the Folktale*, which was first published in 1928, translated into English in 1958 and into French in 1973, dates which demonstrate the originality of Propp's thought. Analysing the contents of a hundred Russian folk-tales Propp finds recurrent themes. Thus:

(1) A king gives an eagle to a hero. The eagle carries off the hero to another kingdom.
(2) An old man gives a horse to Susenko. The horse carries Susenko off to another kingdom.
(3) A sorcerer gives Ivan a boat. The boat carries Ivan off to another kingdom.

(4) A princess gives Ivan a ring. From the ring there emerge young people who carry Ivan off to another kingdom.

There are obvious elements of kinship in the four themes: the names and the attributes of the characters change but their actions and functions are identical. Thus, there are certain functions which constitute unvarying elements of the tale, while the circumstances and the construction are secondary variables. Propp suggests a typology of tales based on these elementary functions, of which he lists 31 that suffice to give a full account of the action of all the tales analysed. Here are eight such functions (as described by C. Brémond in *Communications*, 4, pp. 8–9):

(1) Prologue.
(2) Absence (one of the members of the family is absent).
(3) Prohibition (addressed to the hero).
(4) Transgression (of the prohibition).
(5) Request for information (the wicked character tries to get information).
(6) The information is obtained.
(7) Deception (the evil character tries to deceive his victim).
(8) Involuntary complicity (the victim falls into the trap and aids his enemy), etc.

Propp's analysis has been taken up, and in particular attempts have been made to reduce the number of functions by linking and fusing them. A. J. Greimas counts twenty of them in his *La Sémantique structurale*.

This method of analysis of narrative by reducing it to its basic elements has been applied by Lévi-Strauss to the description and interpretation of myths; following Propp, he shows that meaning resides less in the historical plot than in the structure of its formal constants or mythemes. Here is how he analyses the structure of the Oedipus myth, whose mythemes (narrative elements) he divides into four categories:

(1) Cadmus searches for his sister Europa, who has been raped by Zeus.
Oedipus marries his mother Jocasta.
Antigone violates the prohibition and buries her brother Polynices.

These three mythemes each represent *overvalued kinship*.

(2) The Spartoi kill each other off.
Oedipus kills his father Laius.
Eteocles kills his brother Polynices.

Here what is signified is an *undervalued kinship* relation.

(3) Cadmus kills the dragon.
Oedipus immolates the sphinx.

Monsters are destroyed.

(4) Labdacus means 'lame'.
Laius means 'left'.
Oedipus means 'swollen foot'.

Difficulty in walking.

There is thus a first opposition between (1) and (2): kinship overvalued/undervalued.

If, furthermore, one notes that lame characters in mythology are beings of the earth, the names in category 4 express the autochthony of man; in this they are opposed to the dragon, a chthonic monster whose murder signifies the negation of human autochthony.

The four mythemes therefore constitute a structure:

1/2 = kinship overvalued/undervalued.
3/4 = autochthony denied/claimed

Thus, according to Lévi-Strauss (*Structural Anthropology*), the result is that the fourth category has the same relation to category 3 as category 1 has to category 2:

The impossibility of connecting certain groups of relations is overcome (or more precisely replaced) by the affirmation that two relations which are mutually contradictory are identical in so far as each is, like the other, contradictory with itself. [The myth] would express the impossibility for a society which professes belief in the autochthony of man of passing from this theory to a recognition of the fact that each of us is in reality born of the union of a man and a woman. The difficulty is unsurmountable.

But the myth of Oedipus offers a kind of logical instrument which enables a bridge to be built between the initial problem—is one born of a single person or of two people?—and the associated problem which can be roughly expressed: is like born of like or of other? In this way a correlation becomes clear: the overvaluation of blood relations is to the underestimation of the same, as the effort to escape from autochthony is to the impossibility of succeeding in so doing. Experience can invalidate the theory, but social life verifies cosmology to the extent that both betray the same contradictory structure. Thus the cosmology is true . . .

The problem posed by Freud in 'Oedipal' terms is doubtless no longer that of the alternative between autochthony and sexual reproduction. But it is still a matter of comprehending how *one* can be born of two; how can it be that we have not a single progenitor but a mother *and* a father?

There should be no hesitation in counting Freud, with Sophocles, as one of the sources of the Oedipus myth.

Their versions merit the same credit as other older, and apparently more authentic, versions.

From this analysis—which is unfortunately too condensed to do justice to its methodology—we should bear in mind the possibility of reducing a text to elements whose meaning resides less in their historical content than in the formal system of relations which they constitute.

Literary criticism has imported this method, very much in fashion nowadays, and has extrapolated from it a way of studying narrative, film, and comic strips.

The reader may usefully consult the articles which have appeared in the journal *Communications* (in particular numbers 4, 8 and 11) and the recent (1970) monographs by A. J. Greimas, *Du sens, Essais sémiotiques*; by Julia Kristeva, *Semeiötikê, Recherches pour une sémanalyse*; and by Roland Barthes, *S/Z Essai*. In his essay, a close textual interpretation of Balzac's *Sarrasine*, Barthes shows how the text generates a multiplicity of readings supported by a set of codes superimposed and dovetailed into one another: the *voice of Empiricism*, the *voice of Truth*, the *voice of Science*, the *voice of the Individual*.

The aim of criticism is to liberate the text and to restore its semantic richness by reconstituting the codes and the modes of signification which subtend it.

5

Social codes

Under the heading of logical and aesthetic codes, we have so far considered the relations of man to nature. The individual becomes part of society and his experience is both objective and subjective. One might hold that society is simply a particular element of the world which we live in, and that what has been said of various codes applies equally to social signification and communication.

There is, however, an important difference. The sciences and the arts, as we have defined them so far, aim at communicating experience which is proper to the sender but in which the receiver is not directly implicated. Social communication, on the other hand, deals with the relations between people, and consequently implicates sender and receiver. Society is a system of relations between individuals: its aims are procreation, defence, exchange, production, etc. To this end, the situation of individuals within the group and of groups within the community must be signified. Such is the role of the *insignia* and *signs* which indicate membership of a social category: clan, family, profession, association, etc. Rites, ceremonies, festivals, fashions and games are ways of communicating, by means of which the individual defines himself in relation to the group and the group in relation to society. At the same time they manifest the role which the individual plays and the significance he has.

Science and knowledge are organizers and signifiers of the natural world; social codes are organizers and signifiers of society. What they signify are men or groups and their relations. But man is the vehicle and the substance of the sign, he is both the signifier and the signified; in fact, he is a sign and therefore a convention. Social life is a game in which the individual plays his own role: the patriarch, the tutelary uncle, the prodigal son, or the faithful friend. The social sign, on the other hand, is generally a sign of 'participation' in the sense that we defined above (p. 14). By means of it the individual manifests his identity and his adherence to the group, but at the same time he institutes and voluntarily assumes such adherence.

Social experience—like the experience of nature—has dual characteristics: it is both logical and affective. The former type include signs which indicate the place of the individual and of the group in the hierarchy. Signs which express emotions and sentiments felt by the individual or the group in relation to other individuals or groups are affective.

Didactically speaking, it would therefore be legitimate to reintroduce the scheme utilized so far by distinguishing logical social signs and aesthetic (affective) social signs. In practice, however, the two modes of signification dovetail very closely with one another. This is because the 'sciences of man' are still at an early stage of development, and our knowledge in that domain is based on 'primitive thinking' in which the boundary between science and art is ill-defined. Furthermore, it is clear that there is a more powerful affective relation between man and man than between man and nature, except in the case of the anthropomorphism of religion and archaic cultures. We shall therefore abandon any attempt at precise distinction between science and art where social life is concerned, and we shall, instead, examine the problem from the point of view of signs and of codes.

1 Signs

One of the basic conditions of social life is knowing whom one is dealing with and, therefore, being able to recognize individual and group identity. This is the function of insignia.

(1) SIGNS OF IDENTITY: INSIGNIA

Insignia are marks which indicate the adherence of an individual to a social group. Their function is to express the organization of society and the relation between individuals and groups.

(a) Coats of arms, flags, totems, etc. indicate belonging to a family or clan. They can extend to larger groupings: city, province, nation.

(b) Uniforms, similarly, are signs of a group:

- *(i)* a social group: nobility, bourgeoisie, working class, etc.
- *(ii)* institutional group: army, church, university, etc.
- *(iii)* occupational group: butchers, cooks, carpenters, etc.
- *(iv)* cultural group: sports club, music society, etc.
- *(v)* ethnic group: Bretons, Alsatians, Auvergnats, etc.

(c) Insignia and decorations are symbolic vestiges of arms and uniforms and have the same function in a vestigial fashion. *Decorations* perpetuate the ancient chivalric orders. *Insignia* are evidence of belonging to all kinds of different groups and associations.

(d) Tattooings, make-up, hair-styles, etc. in primitive

societies are codified insignia which, in our society, survive in the form of fashions.

(e) Names and nicknames are the simplest and most universal marks of identity. They are in principle always motivated and designate an individual by his belonging to a family or clan or profession (Sartre 'the tailor'; Lefevre 'the artisan') or a physical category (Leblanc 'white'; Leborgne 'one-eyed'). In contemporary culture this system has broken down and has been replaced by nicknames.

Coats of arms, uniforms, insignia and tattooings are thus ways of distinguishing and, sometimes, of classifying and defining the various groups which constitute society. As Lévi-Strauss has shown with respect to totems, they are essentially social taxonomies. Furthermore, within each group designated by a totem they structure the hierarchies and the internal organization of the group. Such is the function of plumes, crowns, ermine and stripes.

(f) Shop-signs designate socialized objects rather than groups of individuals. In the era before houses were numbered, each building was identified by its sign, a tradition which now exists only in the case of certain commercial enterprises. Such signs like coats of arms are generally iconic (see above p. 26): the bootmaker's boot, the barber's pole, etc. And there are so many inns still called 'The White Horse' or 'The Golden Lion', which hark back to the days of the mail-coach.

The division of cities into districts and streets forms another sign system. In many cultures, castes and professions are grouped in certain districts with a Potters' Row or Weavers' Lane, etc. The accidents of history have generally played havoc with the old street system of contemporary cities; but it may be artificially reconstituted, as in Nice, where there is a Musicians' district in which all the streets are named after famous musicians. New York uses a rationalized system in which the *streets* run at right angles to the *avenues*, and both are simply numbered.

(g) Trade marks indicate and guarantee the origin of a commodity. This goes back to the old artisans: the potter and the furniture maker 'sign' their work; the animal breeder brands his animals, etc.

The multiplication and diversification of commodities and the development of commerce and advertising pose the problem in new terms. The choice of a brand name is determined in such a complex way that manufacturers turn to sociologists, psychologists and even computers. Presentation and packing have taken on a very important semiological value in modern business. In short, what we have grouped under the heading of insignia are signs whose function is to distinguish and identify the component units of social organization and of the topography and economy which underpin it.

(2) THE SIGNS OF POLITE BEHAVIOUR

Signs of identity indicate adherence to a group or function. And for the purposes of communication signs and insignia are ways of making known who one is. But in addition to permanent relations there are transitory ones which vary according to circumstances.

Putting on or not putting on special kinds of clothes to go and visit someone indicates not only the nature of the invitation but also the relations between guest and host, which are also expressed by gestures and other physical attributes.

We have already referred (p. 49) to matters of prosody, kinesics and proxemics, to which we must now add: greetings, insults, feeding, etc.

(a) Tone of voice is one of the most universal ways of signifying the relation between sender and receiver: it can be 'familiar', 'respectful', 'ironic', 'imperative', 'honied', and so on.

(b) Greetings and expressions of politeness play an identical role, and are distinguished by their particularly conventional nature and their variations from culture to culture.

(c) Insults are negative forms of greeting and signs of hostility. There is an amazing variety of them, but they are nevertheless conventional. A challenge is a codified and ritualized form of insult.

(d) Kinesics—literally the study of movements—is an analysis of mimicry, gestures and dances. Gestures and mime are, like intonation and variations of tone of voice, ancillary to language. The study of gesture has a long history, and Darwin was the author of a work on the expression of emotion in man and animal (1873). But it was Ray Birdwhistell's *Introduction to Kinesics* in 1952 that marked the beginning of a systematic study of bodily gestures with a science dealing with 'the communicative aspects of the acquired and structural behaviour of body movements.' Here is Birdwhistell's account of the properties of kinesic signs based on a linguistic model (quoted in *Langages*, vol. 10, June 1968):

> There are several varieties of kinesic signs:
> *pronominal* ones are associated with substitutes for pronouns structured according to the opposition distance/proximity: *he/me, this/that*, etc. The same gesture in a more expansive manner pluralizes the pronominal kinesic sign and thus gives: we, them, etc.

In a similar way one can distinguish *verboid* signs of *tense*, for example, associated with uninterrupted-movement pronominal signs. Signs of *place* should also be noted: above, below, behind, in front of, through, etc.

In a similar way the various elements of dance have been analysed and codified. For all these matters, which go beyond the limits of the present essay, those interested may usefully consult volume number 10 of the journal *Langages* (June 1968) which is devoted to gestural behaviour and languages.

(e) Proxemics. Linguistic communication uses not only gestures but also space and time; thus the distance that we place between ourselves and the person we are talking to, and the time we take to consider or reply to his remarks, in themselves constitute signs. These are the signs which are studied under the name of proxemics.

The 'language' of proxemics is particularly interesting because, although like all sign systems it is conventionalized, it varies from culture to culture and thus may give rise to numerous misunderstandings. The fundamental work in this respect is E. T. Hall's *The Silent Language* (1959). According to Hall there are eight significant distances between typical American speakers (see Table 5).

The distance is thought to be determined by acoustic reasons but is in fact more a matter of convention: the English and Americans 'keep a polite distance' between speakers; Latins tend to reduce it. The result is that the former tend to feel constrained and attacked by the latter, who find them cold and distant. As Hall puts it:

> In Latin America the distance is smaller than in the United States. In fact, people cannot speak comfortably unless they are very close, a closeness

TABLE 5

(1) Very close (5 to 20 cm)	Slight whisper	Very secret
(2) Close (20 to 30 cm)	Audible whisper	Confidential
(3) Fairly close (30 to 50 cm)	Low voice indoors Full voice outdoors	Confidential
(4) Neutral (50 to 90 cm)	Low voice, low intensity	Personal subject
(5) Neutral (1·30 to 1·50 m)	Full voice	Impersonal subject
(6) Public distance (1·60 to 2·40 m)	Full voice with slight emphasis	Public information intended for people other than person spoken to
(7) Across a room (2·40 to 6 m)	Loud voice	Speaking to a group
(8) Beyond these limits (from 6 to 30 m)	Loud voice	Greetings at a distance, departures, etc.

which evokes aggressive or erotic intent in the USA. The result is that when they approach we move away, and they think that we are distant, cold, reserved and unfriendly. We, in turn, perpetually accuse them of cornering us, of breathing down our necks, or of spluttering all over us.

Americans who have lived in Latin America for some time use subterfuges: they barricade themselves behind their desks and use furniture to keep the Latin-American at what they consider to be a comfortable distance. The result is often that the Latin-American may go so far as to climb over the various obstacles until he reaches a distance that he finds comfortable.

No less significant is the waiting-period imposed upon a visitor. The least of bureaucrats would feel he had gone down in the world were he not able to impose a delay in conformity with his rank and dignity. Such delays also vary from culture to culture and from situation to situation. An ambassador to the Great Mogul sometimes had to wait three months before being granted an audience. And it is well-known that women accept the homage of their admirers only after a subtly calculated delay.

Space and time play a significant role in ceremonies, processions and banquets. Space is an indicator of the relations between speakers, relations which are more or less 'distant' or 'intimate'.

(f) Food is an important mode of group identification and manners. It is often surrounded by taboos. The preparation and serving of meals are regulated by a system of conventions. To refuse an aperitif is, in certain French milieux, still a strongly felt insult.

The semiological function of food survives in our feasts and banquets, as well as in a number of taboos and customs. Tea in England is pervaded by a ritual which bears traces of its Eastern origin.

(g) How can one bring this inventory to a close? Everything is a sign: presents, our houses, our furniture, our domestic animals.

(3) THE NATURE OF SOCIAL SIGNS

We have seen that signs can be more or less specialized, i.e. structured and conventional. In contemporary culture social signs are, generally speaking, less rather than more conventional. Such is the case for our name systems, insignia and signs as compared with highly elaborate systems such as totems, coats of arms, and the clothes worn by castes, professions or clans in other cultures.

Another characteristic of signs is their arbitrariness or their motivation. Most social signs are of the motivated type, either by metaphor, or often by metonymy. They are allegorical images: the scales and sword of justice; the bowed head or the kissing of the hand which stand for 'homage'. But they often survive in a degraded symbolic form whose original sense is lost.

They are highly connotative, expressing force, power or humility, values which often have their source in a symbolism rooted in the collective unconscious. For these reasons they are more often aesthetic than logical in type, although in principle the majority are classificatory signs. But because of their archaic origin their modes of signification are prescientific, analogical or homo-analogical (cf. above, p. 34). They are, furthermore, extremely sensitive to the mechanism of the recurrence of the signifier upon the signified. It is not uncommon for the form of coats of arms, names, or mottoes to generate pseudo-historical fables which have often been noted in archaic literature and myth. Lévi-Strauss, in particular, has shown how totemic naming-systems (which are taxonomic) by analogy generate taboos, prohibitions, or clan relations underpinned by eponymous legends which are thus grafted on to the stock of natural relations between wolf, snake, bear or frog.

Social signs are iconic in nature, and are related to aesthetic signs. This is no accident, for in social communication the sender, more often than not, is both the bearer of the sign and at the same time its referent. This confusion of subject and object can only encourage the contamination of the referential and the emotive function.

2 Codes

Clothes, food, gestures, distances, and so on, are signs which, in various proportion and according to diverse modalities, are ingredients in the various types of social communication. These take innumerable forms: rituals, feasts, ceremonies, protocols, codes of conventional polite behaviour, games. Four main categories can be distinguished: (1) *protocols*, the function of which is to set up communication among individuals; (2) *rituals*, in which it is the group itself that acts as emitter; (3) *fashions*, which are stylized and individualized samples of codings; and (4) *games*—private and individual or public and collective— which are representations of a social situation.

(1) PROTOCOLS

Society groups individuals according to the actions they undertake together. Each individual has his place and his function; each is defined in society by his family, religious and professional relations with others into which he enters. It is indispensable that these relations should be recognized and identified. Such is, as we have seen, the function of names, nicknames, insignia, signs, coats of arms and, quite particularly, clothing. Furthermore, when individuals get together with a view to some collective action their relations must be signified: who it is that commands and who obeys, who gives and who receives, who invites whom, etc. Protocol and etiquette regulate the position of each person in a procession or round a table. We know how the Knights of the Round Table solved the problem, and the role it played in the recent Vietnam Conference.

The function of salutations and greetings is formally to initiate and terminate communications, and even in so doing the relation between the parties must be indicated: equality, superiority or inferiority, friendship, hostility or indifference, desire for or rejection of communication.

Titles, formulae—in certain cases even invective and insults—tone of voice, gesture and attitude together constitute a codified *ensemble*, the conventional character of which becomes evident when one tries to translate them from one language to another or from one culture to another.

Good manners and *savoir-vivre* are signs by means of which an individual manifests his belonging to a group. This knowledge of and respect for the customs, passwords or special signs of the group are what make him, in the eyes of the group, a man-of-the-world, or of the underworld.

(2) RITUALS

Ritual is a mode of group communication; the ritual message is emitted both by and in the name of the community. The sender is the group, not the individual.

It is through the intermediary of its religious cult that the society communes with the gods. Etymologically *religio* means *link*; a link both between the group and its divinity and amongst the faithful themselves. *Family* or *national cults* are, in the same way, forms of communication with ancestors or with the fatherland. They are almost always religious in origin and always bear the stamp of religiosity. The ceremonies which accompany *pacts, treaties and alliances* set the seal on intergroup relations that exchange obligations, services, goods, women, etc. Initiation, coronation, sacramental and funerary ritual institute relations between the individual and the group which thus receives him or her into its midst.

In all such rituals, the emitter is the group, either the group as a whole or those officiants to whom it has delegated its powers. But the group always participates, either by virtue of its presence, or as expressed in the songs, prayers, silences, plaudits, hurrahs of the individuals participating in the communication. Such participation may be prolonged in the forms of ritual ceremonies whose form is itself prescribed by the code. Solemn commemorative festivities may function as reminders of an initial agreement and as a confirmation of the bonds inaugurated by it.

The function of ritual is not so much to inform as to commune. Its aim is to demonstrate the solidarity of individuals relative to religious, national or social obligations contracted by the community. And it does this by means of sign systems which, whatever their historical or pseudo-historical origins and whatever their graphic value, are always highly conventionalized.

(3) FASHIONS

Fashions are ways of being common to a group: ways of dressing, eating or housing. They take on great importance in a society in which superabundance of consumer commodities frees the latter from their primary function (that of protection or nourishment) and allows them to function simply as the signs of social status. Such is very evidently the case as far as concerns, for example, our ties, cars, and Regency furniture.

Fashion proceeds by a double centripetal and centrifugal movement. The desire for identification with a high-prestige group leads one to adopt those signs by which that group is known. But those same signs are consequently abandoned by the members of the groups who refuse the identification. This is one of the mechanisms which renders fashion so fluid and creative, particularly in cultures in which social signs are weakly codified. Fashion, like entertainment, compensates for some frustrations, and satisfies desire for prestige and power.

(4) GAMES

Like art, games are imitations of reality, particularly of social reality. They are situations which are constructed with a view to placing individuals in a socially significant set-up. The *arts* imitate life with a view to placing the receiver face to face with reality and with a view to making him feel, through the mediation of the image, the emotions and sentiments aroused by that reality. *Games* mimic real life with a view to placing the receiver within reality and making him, through the mediation of the image, enact aspects of that reality. Entertainments may be both games and arts: games from the point of view of the actor, arts from the point of view of the spectator.

Games can be classified according to the three principal modes of experience: intellectual/scientific; practical/social; affective/aesthetic. The first class comprises all construction-type games, including verbal constructions such as puns, riddles and crosswords, in which the player gives meaning to an amorphous reality by structuring it. The activity of the child doing a puzzle is of the same order as that of the herbalist identifying and classifying plants. The second class comprises those which place the player in a social situation: family, work, war, etc.: the little girl playing at being mummy, chess playing, or Rugby players imitating war, etc. From the point of view of the spectator, watching sport supplies the third type: supporters follow the changing fortunes of the game like citizens of a besieged city watching their garrison from the ramparts. In most games all three functions play a part.

The function of games is learning and selection: the child playing mummy or soldiers is learning a role; the tournament enables the strongest and most worthy to be selected for the functions of leadership. Games of chance symbolize the struggle of the individual against destiny, though in situations from which the dangers of reality have generally been extracted.

Furthermore, games have an entertainment function in that they are able to satisfy, in a sublimated way, desires which have been frustrated in real life: desire for power, gain, social status, etc. Contemporary psychoanalysis and psychiatry have cast light on this matter, and have extended the concept of games by showing that games, like art, express cultural archetypes with roots in the individual and collective unconsciousness.

In this perspective, the notion of a game, that is of the imitation of a social situation, has been extended to many aspects of our behaviour. Psychological disequilibrium goes hand in hand with disturbed communication, and psychosomatic medicine has shown that disturbances of the higher mental functions have organic consequences. Everything we do has a meaning; but to the extent that the relation between signifier and signified is irrational or unconscious the meaning requires interpretation. Modern educational psychology teaches us that the rebellious, lying, runaway child is trying to communicate something and to establish a different relation to his environment. This is not restricted to childhood. In a popular work entitled *Games People Play* (New York, 1964) Dr Eric Berne, an American psychiatrist, demonstrates that our social and particularly our family behaviour can usefully be conceptualized as 'games', that is to say, systems of relations that reproduce former situations of which the 'players' are unaware: they enact roles such as that of the domestic tyrant, the frigid woman, the alcoholic, or the gambler, the deeper meanings of which remain obscure to them. Dr Berne makes an inventory of such game situations and of their rules.

Here is a summary of a widely played marriage game called 'If it weren't for you'. The players are a 'timid' wife married to a domestic 'tyrant'. The wife complains bitterly of the restrictions imposed by the husband on her freedom; if it weren't for him she would travel, work, dance, ride, and so on. In fact experience shows that the wife would in any case be unable to assume any freedom, even if she were given it. The 'tyrant' is thus doing her a favour by keeping her from situations in which she would be faced with any such decision. It is for this reason that such a woman often marries precisely that kind of man.

This 'game' with its roles, its situations and its characters constitutes a perfectly stereotyped drama with few variations. Thus, below their multifarious surface 'games' are more or less conventionalized sign-systems. Their essential trait is that the *sender*, i.e. the player himself or herself, constitutes the sign: to play is to be someone else. The *doll* is the 'child' and the *player* is the 'mother'; the pawns, rooks, etc. of chess are 'armies', and the players are rival strategists.

All activity tends to become a game to the extent that it loses its immediate function, e.g. hunting or paper warfare. In the category of games a special place must be given to *dramatic* games; décor, stage sets, and actors are the signs.

Given that games are sign-systems, they are necessarily codified either in a figurative or in an ideosemic way. The total absence of rules would render the players, toys and phases of the game quite meaningless. Thus, wrestling in its rule-less form is not a sporting game, as Barthes has shown (*Mythologies*), and that is why the outcome is decided in advance by the organizers; it is, however, a dramatic game with prescribed roles: the Traitor, the Evil One, the Innocent; and with prescribed situations: evil meets retribution, courage is recompensed.

Protocols, rites, games: everything in social life is a sign, and above all the participant individuals are signs. In the protocols, we 'play our part': patriarch, prodigal son, faithful friend, or martyr for the Mother Country. In our games we play a role. The limit between the two is not easy to define.

Semiologically the problem of games, like that of the arts, is double: on the one hand there is a morphology the object of which is to reduce each game to its 'immediate constituents' with a view to classifying and defining their functions, i.e. the rules by which they combine. On the other hand, there is a semantic (and symbolic) problem of establishing the social function and meaning of these elementary units of games (ludemes) within the myths and the general culture that are the basis for and background to the games people play.

Conclusion: mythologies of our times

The notion of *image* is one of the key concepts of our culture. Everybody has one: actors, politicians, women; and the least amongst us is concerned to maintain and not to compromise his image. Whether it be that of the watchful father, the faithful husband, the good citizen or man-about-town, the carefully constructed image is jealously protected.

Mythologies express a vision of man and the world, and signify a way of organizing the cosmos and society. And if they disintegrate into contingent notions they enable one to discern beneath accidental variations certain stable and well-structured systems of meaning.

When one talks of myth one generally thinks of archaic primitive cultures, of prelogical thought-forms; and it is true that in such closed, stabilized cultures mythic codes are easy to observe. In the same way it is there that one finds simple static forms of ritual social codes which go back to distant history and are rooted in the collective unconscious.

Contemporary society, on the other hand, *seems* freer, and established on a rational basis. However, this is far from really being the case. The life of someone such as President Kennedy, for example, is strewn with omens, trials, miraculous gifts, and all the signs that typify the mythic hero. In this respect his death, too, fits a pattern: despite an enquiry which came to the conclusion that his murderer was an isolated unbalanced individual, public opinion rejects such an accidental end which would deprive him of a meaningful destiny, and insists that the hero was betrayed: betrayal is one of the major themes of epic literature.

Modern science bears witness to this semiological aspect of our attitudes and beliefs. Pavlov's dogs do not react to things but to their signs, and behaviourism claims that our behaviour is conditioned by signs. For psychoanalysis, moreover, these signs stem from archaic, unconscious and irrational situations. Certain of these, according to Jung's theory of archetypes, are common to the group, whilst others are proper to the individual, as Freud with his analysis of complexes would have us believe. Finally, psycho-sociological surveys based on statistical analysis of replies to verbal tests and questionnaires lead one to interpret sign-systems in terms of the tendencies characteristic of groups and situations. So it would seem that most of our choices—even those most freely or at least most rationally taken—are in fact conditioned by unconscious mythical constructs.

Why do we drink wine or milk? Where does the French love of steak and chips come from? What are the origins of our foibles and prejudices? Roland Barthes tries to answer such questions in his collection of essays entitled *Mythologies* (pp. 59–60):

> To believe in wine is a coercive collective act. A Frenchman who kept this myth at arm's length would expose himself to minor but definite problems of integration, the first of which, precisely, would be that

of having to explain his attitude. The universality principle fully applies here, inasmuch as society calls anyone who does not believe in wine by names such as sick, disabled or depraved; it does not *comprehend* him (in both senses, intellectual and spatial, of the word). Conversely, an award of good integration is given to whoever is a practising wine-drinker; knowing *how* to drink is a national technique which serves to qualify the Frenchman, to demonstrate at once his performance, his control and his sociability. Wine thus gives a foundation for a collective morality, within which everything is redeemed: excesses, misfortunes and crimes are no doubt possible with wine, but never viciousness, treachery or baseness; the evil it can generate is in the nature of fate and therefore escapes penalization; it evokes the theatre rather than a basic temperament.

Wine is part of society because it provides a basis not only for a morality but also for an environment; it is an ornament in the slightest ceremonials of French daily life, from the snack (wine and cheese) to the feast, from the conversation of the local café to the speech at a formal dinner. It exalts all climates, of whatever kind: in cold weather, it is associated with all the myths of becoming warm; and at the height of summer, with all the images of shade, with all things cool and sparkling. There is no situation involving some constraint (temperature, hunger, boredom, compulsion, or disorientation) which does not give rise to dreams of wine. Combined as a basic substance with other alimentary figures, it can cover all the aspects of space and time for the Frenchman. As soon as one gets to know someone's daily life fairly well, the absence of wine gives a sense of shock like something exotic.

M. Coty, having allowed himself to be photographed

at the beginning of his seven years' presidency, sitting
at home before a table on which a bottle of beer
seemed to replace, by an extraordinary exception, the
familiar litre of red wine, the whole nation was in a
flutter; it was as intolerable as having a bachelor king.
Wine is here part of state policy.

Barthes shows that there is thus a mythology of milk, of
steak and chips, of the automobile, of holidays, of literature,
and so on. And it is evident that all the excellent and most
sincere reasons which we give in justification of our tastes,
desires and judgments are entirely irrational. This is in fact
known to and used by modern advertising. Countless
examples of this can be found in Vance Packard's classic
The Hidden Persuaders (1957). The manufacturers of
margarine, for example, were from the first, and still are
now, up against a tenacious prejudice against their commodity which compared to butter is said to be 'fatty', 'heavy
and indigestible', and to have an 'oily taste'. One need only
disguise margarine as butter, or butter as margarine to find
out that most people are taken in by appearances and
attribute to butter the defects of margarine and to margarine
the virtues of butter. The same is true of the majority of
products which nowadays are quite standardized and
homogenized, to the extent that there is practically no
objective difference between different brands of toothpaste,
shampoo, or washing powder.

Given this fact, how does one explain the attachment of
the smoker to his brand of cigarettes, since experience has
shown that in most cases he is quite unable to distinguish it
from other brands? The conclusion drawn by experts in
these matters is unanimous: people choose a brand of
cigarettes according to the image which the brand has. It is
equally clear that women buy cosmetics not for their
'softening', 'astringent' or 'rejuvenating' properties but as a

result of the image of youth, success or love which they advertise. Hence the importance of name and packaging and of all which goes to make what is called the 'brand image'. Business sells symbols. And these symbols function at quite irrational subconscious and unconscious levels.

Here is the success story of the prune told by Vance Packard (*The Hidden Persuaders*, pp. 119–20):

In the 1950s, the unfortunate prune wasn't selling very well despite all the efforts of the corporation, which as a last resort took it to the Institute of Motivational Research for psychotherapy. The patient was found to be suffering from an acute inferiority complex.

Verbal association tests showed that in people's minds the prune was linked to words like 'dried out', 'old maid', 'boarding-house', and above all to 'constipation'. What was needed was an entirely new image.

From one day to the next the prune became a delicious soft fruit, almost a sweet, if advertising were to be believed. The new image showed prunes in an environment as far removed as possible from the sombre, old-maidish surroundings in which four black prunes stagnated in some dismal liquid. The new advertisements used brilliant gay colours and the silhouettes of youthful figures playing. Subsequently these images changed from children to pretty girls skating or playing tennis. And wherever the prune appeared it was on a background of white or on brightly coloured plates. These images were accompanied by captions such as 'Fly into the air', 'The world is yours', 'Prunes put colour in your cheeks'. The prune's success was a veritable Cinderella fairy tale.

The ideas of *image*, *message* and *manipulation* of public opinion by means of an understanding of its 'deep motivation' are keys to contemporary culture spreading from America to Europe. It has moved from the domain of advertising and has invaded politics and social relations. Stars, politicians and little by little everyone else has an 'image' which is patiently constructed and carefully maintained. Elections are handed over to advertising agencies, and the image of the candidate is artificially constructed from head to foot. We live in an age of the image.

The 'opium of the people' today takes the form of political, cultural and economic propaganda, whose most effective weapon and most insidious illusion is to persuade us that signs really are the things they claim to be; just as we persuade ourselves that we are 'ourselves', signs amongst signs in this theatre in which we play our own role.

Kings were formerly thought to be the sons of the gods sent down to represent them on earth; today presidents are the creatures of television projected on the magic screen between margarine and hungry enzymes. But at least we are beginning to understand that our lives are packed with signs, and to become aware of their nature and power. This semiological awareness could become the main guarantor of our liberty.

Select bibliography

BARTHES, R., *Mythologies*, Paris, 1957 (see also *Communications* no. 4); *Mythologies*, London 1972.
— *Système de la mode*, Paris, 1967.
— *S/Z Essai*, Paris, 1970.
BERNE, E., *Games People Play*, New York, 1964.
BUYSSENS, E., *Le Langage et le discours. Essai de linguistique fonctionelle dans le cadre d'une sémiologie*, Brussels, 1943.
DE SAUSSURE, F., *General Course in Linguistics*, London, 1973.
FOUCAULT, M., *Les Mots et les choses, une archéologie des sciences humaines*, Paris, 1966; *Order of Things: Archaeology of the Human Sciences*, London, 1970.
FRYE, N., *Anatomy of Criticism*, Princeton, 1957.
GREIMAS, A. J., *La Sémantique structurale*, Paris, 1966.
— *Du sens, Essais sémiologiques*, Paris, 1970.
GUIRAUD, P., *La Sémantique* ('Que sais-je?' series, no. 655), Paris, 1955.
— *Essais de stylistique*, Paris, 1970.
HALL, E. T., *The Silent Language*, New York, 1959.
KRISTEVA, J., *Semeiötikê, Recherches pour une sémanalyse*, Paris, 1970.
Langages, no. 10, 'Pratiques et langages gestuels', Paris, 1968.
LÉVI-STRAUSS, C., *La Pensée sauvage*, Paris, 1962; *The Savage Mind*, London, 1966.
— *Anthropologie structurale*, Paris, 1958; *Structural Anthropology*, London, 1968.

MCLUHAN, M., *Understanding Media*, New York, 1964.

MORRIS, C. W., *Signs, Language and Behavior*, New York, 1946.

MOUNIN, G., 'Les systèmes de communication non-linguistiques', *BSLP*, 44, 1959.

— *Problèmes théoriques de la traduction*, Paris, 1963.

— 'Recherches sémiologiques', *Communications*, no. 4, Paris, 1964.

PACKARD, V., *The Hidden Persuaders*, London, 1957.

PEIRCE, C. S., *Philosophical Writings of Peirce*, New York, 1940.

PIKE, K. L., *Language in Relation to a Unified Theory of the Structure of Human Behavior*, Glendale, California, 1955.

PRIETO, L. J., *Messages et signaux*, Paris, 1966.

PROPP, V., *Morphology of the Folktale*, Indiana, 1958. (The original Russian edition dates from 1928.)

Semiotica, Journal of the International Association for Semiotic Studies, The Hague.